MILL POND CHURCH

The Crucified Church!

Leading Your Church through Death & Rebirth

I have been crucified with Christ and I no longer live, but Christ lives in me. The life I live in the body, I live by faith in the Son of God, who loved me and gave himself for me (Galatians 2:20).

Pastor Joel L. Rissinger
3/12/2010

Blessings

Endorsements

"**W**ow! With fearless wisdom earned through years of experience, Joel Rissinger has boldly tackled a tough issue head on. This is a very important book that church leaders in the United States need to read."

Dr. Dave Earley, Director and Chair, Pastoral Leadership and Church Planting, Liberty Baptist Theological Seminary

"Joel Rissinger's book is not only a fast-paced journey through his rich experience in pastoral ministry, but a fresh blueprint for spiritual revitalization. The reader can instantly feel his passion for building healthy and vibrant congregations in the face of increasing biblical ignorance. You will emerge from the "ride" appreciative of his no-nonsense but loving approach."

Joseph Tkach, D.Min., President, Grace Communion International and author of the book, *Transformed by Truth*, the story of the reformation of the Worldwide Church of God

"One of the hardest things to do is to kill a small, struggling church. The bias of the few remaining members is to push on, under the charge of faithfulness, hoping something will change. Joel Rissinger is right: death is often the biblical pathway to life. He shows us how, with passionate and practical advice, to transform a church to the vibrancy it once knew."

Dr. Tom Nebel, Director of Church Planting, Converge Worldwide and author of the book, *Church Parenting Landmines* and co-author of *Church Planting Landmines*

"Joel Rissinger is one of my heroes. He deeply understands the centrality of the church in God's plan and is totally committed to it, as evidenced by the content of this book. Only someone who loves the church as much as Joel could get away with using such radical images to communicate how to think better about the church. Ignore his insights and you are taking the risk of truly killing your church."

Dr. Stephen Kemp, Founding Academic Dean of the Antioch School of Church Planting and Leadership Development.

"Joel Rissinger's assessment of the church in the early twenty-first century is candidly honest. He presents the startling reality that the church is losing ground in the United States and through many US churches the power of the Gospel to change lives looks impotent at best. Rissinger's proposal for change is a biblical proposal for following Christ not just personally but corporately."

Rev. Clark Pfaff, Pastor, Valley Brook Community Church

"Joel is not merely a theorist examining the issue of church health from afar or a blogger standing on a soapbox. Joel is a daily practitioner having both lived through the stress of an unhealthy situation and the joy of starting again in a new one. This book may be the catalyst needed to help hundreds of churches awaken from and shake off the stranglehold of dead and dying formalism and tradition."

Will Marotti, Senior Pastor, New Life Church

This Book is sure to challenge, inspire, infuriate, and otherwise shake up an American church that has become far too complacent in the face of the increasing irrelevance of its message and practice. If you're concerned about the state of the church and the watered down "gospel" in so much of

American evangelicalism, this book is for you. But be warned: Pastor Rissinger throws down the gauntlet in this book, and if you aren't prepared to take a good, hard look at what your church has been doing, you will want to steer clear of it. For those who are up to the challenge, though, the book provides tested ideas that can lead to "life from the dead" for congregations stuck in a rut. You may not agree with everything here, and some of it may not be relevant in your situation, but you're sure to be stretched and challenged to think through what you are doing in your church, why you're doing it, and whether it really is advancing the Kingdom. And you'll catch a glimpse of a new vision for what the church can be if we have the courage to forget what lies behind and to press on ahead, pursuing God's best for His people in our day.

Dr. Glenn Sunshine, author of *Why You Think the Way You Do: The Story of Western Worldviews from Rome to Home*

"This is a dangerous book. Read it at your own risk. Some books bring joy; some cause tears; and others lead me to pray. God has used Joel to write a book that does all three. You will laugh, you will cry, and I pray you will end up on your knees. So be careful....this book may change your ministry."

Paul Hubley, District Executive Minister, Converge Northeast

To my wife Karen—you are a blessing from God and, for me, the perfect model of what Jesus wants for all of us, his Bride, the Church.

To my son David—my firstborn, intelligent beyond your years. Thank you for your love and constant challenge to keep me honest and on track.

To my daughter Shelly—my baby girl, who's not a baby anymore. Your love of Jesus and willingness to risk all to share Him makes me more proud than you'll ever know.

To the elders, leaders, and much-loved members of Mill Pond Church. You are the best spiritual family I could ever dream of or imagine. Thanks for the honor of being your pastor!

To so many fellow pastors and leaders who have encouraged me and given me support for this work… thank you so much! I'm blessed to have friends like you!

The Crucified Church!

Foreword

This book is for pastors, church board members, ministry leaders, and denominational executives who care about the bride of Christ. While the title and some of my illustrations may be "edgy," it's my prayer that the ideas expressed will foster discussion, debate, and ultimately, real change.

Everyone is talking about the fate of the modern church. Every pastor I know is afraid for her. Research by George Barna and others has suggested that we're in *big* trouble…in fact, that the very existence of the modern evangelical church is at stake. Seminars, books, and conferences are being offered as solutions to this problem. But have we considered the alternative—that it's actually God's will that the church die…so that she can be reborn? And if it *is* His will, shouldn't we be supporting the idea instead of fighting it?

I must say at the onset that I love the church. It's impossible for me to hear a sermon about the purpose of the church or to read Ephesians chapter 4 without crying. When I think about how Jesus feels about her, I am at once both moved and afraid. I am moved because, after 25 years of marriage to the most wonderful woman I've ever met, I relate to His love for the church. I'm afraid because, while I know He cleanses her (Ephesians 5:26), she's far from perfect now and thus needs to "pick up her cross."

That's my conflict and challenge as I write about the church in her imperfect state; I run the risk of angering Jesus, the protective groom. I know how angry I'd be to hear someone pointing out all the flaws of my bride (although they are few). How do we critique and challenge without offense or sin?

I've changed the names of certain people and places for the sake of grace (for example, "Community Church" is a pseudonym, as are most other church names herein). Still, talking about "crucified" something Jesus loves is a tightrope walk to say the least!

It makes me feel a bit better to consider the impact of the philosophical foundation of this book—death and rebirth. It's the reborn bride I'm looking for and that Scripture speaks of, not the selfish, inwardly focused version often encountered today. It's the bride composed of people who've *truly* been crucified *with* Christ (Galatians 2:20) that comprise the church of the future. My prayer is that this book will foster change and be used by God to help produce that bride through death and rebirth.

To that end,

PJ

Chapter 1

The Church Is Dying…
And She Should!

Community Church (CC) was in many ways the consummate metaphor of the modern evangelical church. Well over 100 years old, she took pride in her history and past accomplishments. She was a church of survivors—people who had weathered the storms of cultural change and decline together.

Started by European immigrants in the 1800s, the church had expanded to represent mostly white, primarily European congregants who moved from the inner city to the suburbs in the 1960s as their original neighborhood became increasingly populated by non-white, non-European families. The move was positioned as an expansion, yet the new sanctuary had fewer seats than her original. The truth is, like so many churches at the time, CC was trying to escape the urbanization and diversification of her city rather than engage it, or act as salt and light.

While her initial suburban growth was impressive, the 10–15 years prior to my arrival had seen the church decline and deteriorate into disharmony and conflict. Some older members would sooner brag about how many pastors they had "gotten rid of," than celebrate souls being won. The pastor I would ultimately replace was driven out because he was unwilling to act as a chaplain instead of being a visionary leader. Chaplains provide religious services and spiritual care. Visionary leaders perform those services, but they also make decisions—sometimes very hard ones. The pastor had implemented contemporary worship music, led the church into more aggressive outreach, and had begun exploring the implementation of an elder-led structure instead of a purely congregational model. This went over like a lead balloon.

Perhaps CC's greatest flaw was that her doggedly inward focus on "discipleship" left little evangelistic and community outreach time or money to spend. This had taken its toll on attendance, budget, and general spiritual development. When a church separates discipleship from evangelism and then emphasizes "teaching" in lieu of outreach, the ironic result is that the members become less spiritually developed. Members weren't given opportunities *through* the church to use what they had learned *in* the church about reaching the lost. (We'll discuss this more in a later chapter.)

As a result, lifelong city residents had rarely even heard of the church, despite her long life in the community. There was no budget for evangelism and, while she spent nearly 20 percent of her budget on "missions," these included efforts often far removed from the evangelization of lost souls. For example, we paid one couple to teach Sunday school classes and lead Bible studies in a church in the Middle East. These activities, while worthwhile, didn't reach the lost. Also, they were jobs that should have been done by indigenous leaders, not missionaries.

Concerned, but not panicked, the leadership of the church decided to explore strategies for growth which would allow the church's "rich heritage" to survive. One of the deacons had read Rick Warren's, *The Purpose- Driven Church* and shared it with others on the Board. "This is it!" they reasoned—"the solution!"

I naively took the bait, agreeing initially to act as interim and then ultimately as Senior Pastor. I believed in the biblical foundation of Matthew 22 and Matthew 28, the Great Commandments and, the Great Commission. I knew that if any church *truly* committed to these as the reason for their existence, they'd become strong and healthy. The problem was that they weren't committed to this.

What I learned, after seven years of struggle is, like so many churches involved in "renewal" projects, they simply wanted a magic pill. They wanted, a *program* which would, when tacked on to their existing identity, values, history, traditions, and dreams—*voila*—make them healthy again. They thought that Rick Warren's book and the programs contained therein would fix them, while essentially leaving everything the same.

Nothing could be more incorrect. As Jesus clearly explained, old wineskins make horrible containers for new wine. I think my move was partially out of ignorance of the true motivations of some members and partially selfish in that I *really* wanted to be successful as the champion of change for God. I also tried so hard to "sell" these changes that I probably refused to see that the necessary commitment was lacking. Still, wanting to believe that they sincerely wanted to change and focus on God's purposes, I attempted to lead them through a seven year transition toward becoming a "Purpose-Driven" church.

Transition we did! We instituted Warren's CLASS 101–401 membership and growth courses. We reworked our budget. We even rewrote our constitution and created an elders-led leadership structure to replace our democratically elected board members. We began outreach programs for the homeless in our city and created an evangelism budget for mailings and other promotions in the city.

Along with transition came the battles—oh, the battles! I should have been prepared for them. You see, prior to my role at CC, I served as a pastor in the Worldwide Church of God and helped three congregations move from cultish heresy to biblical, evangelical doctrine. I *know* the challenge of change! Still, I've joked that it's easier to tell people their church is a cult, and thus virtually everything they've believed is a lie, than it is to convince some churches to ordain elders or change their style of music!

Brutal warfare ensued—but we survived.

Still, growth didn't follow our transition and I was perplexed. I had read Dan Southerland's book, *Transitioning*, and even had lunch with him during a Saddleback Church conference in California. The folks at CC and I followed everything in the Purpose-Driven program to a "*T,*" yet we grew from 150–200 in attendance, and then stalled. Nothing I did caused growth and, despite the changes, nothing *really* changed.

Frustrated, weary, and embroiled in battle with one of my new elders, I went to a pastor's prayer meeting to vent (yes, that's what really happens at those meetings, even though they're often called "prayer meetings"). Many church members would be shocked to learn that (perish the thought) pastors too are human beings who laugh and irreverently joke about their jobs just to stay sane.

In the context of the joking and venting, I commented that all of the problems our churches were experiencing could be solved if we just "merged into one." One of the pastors called my jovial bluff, thus beginning the eventual merger of Community Church, New Born Church, and the Second Spanish Evangelical Church! A new church was born.

If I seem like a glutton for punishment—I truly was. Leading three church congregations from heresy to orthodoxy, taking a 118-year-old traditional church from inwardly focused congregationalism to an elder-led, purpose-driven emphasis wasn't "challenging" enough, I suppose. I had apparently decided to "cap it all off" with a three-way merger and then a new church plant. Wow—I should have been institutionalized! Looking back, I think I needed serious psychological help for even thinking of these scenarios, but I guess this proves that God has a sense of humor –after all, He created me, didn't He?

So we forged ahead…

The merger itself was so Spirit-led that it happened much more rapidly and smoothly than we ever anticipated. In the beginning, up to and immediately after the congregational votes to merge, it was relatively painless. The aftermath, however, resulted in close to two-thirds of our original members leaving, some with anger and outright hostility toward me and the other pastors involved, especially the new senior pastor.

Together, we endured angry emails, emotional meetings, and even thinly-veiled threats for close to two years.

During that time, New Born Church paid our salaries and let us borrow (and sometimes keep) equipment to start Mill Pond Church in Newington, Connecticut, about twenty minutes north of New Born. The stress of the merger and the challenge of our new church plant was a killer combination, kind of an adrenaline cocktail. But in the end—I'd do it all again in a heartbeat.

Why?

Since the merger, the good news is that we've grown dramatically and had a major impact not just on one community, but on three. What was two church sites reaching about 500–600 people, has now, three years later, grown to four locations regularly serving nearly 1,000 people. As I type this, New Born just held a massive Christmas Eve service at a local theater. More than 1,200 attended and dozens responded to an invitation to receive Christ. Though we lost at least 150 of our original attendees, our growth is surging and we've seen hundreds saved. Today, we believe our growth has literally just begun.

Was it worth it? Absolutely, without a doubt! Yet, honestly, was it a true transition? Technically, was it even a "merger" that we experienced? Not really…actually, not at all! In fact, I think I was naïve about mergers and transitions prior to this experience. I, like so many others, believed that it could be done smoothly, peacefully, retaining much of the past, etc.—but it cannot! Our merger was more of a takeover and, ultimately, our "transition" was a death and rebirth.

You see, I believe most church revitalization projects that we read about in religious journals, and elsewhere, are really just mercy killings followed by new birth.

Ironically (or maybe I should say "divinely"), we adopted the name, New Born Church. In fact, that's what happened—CC died and something new was born. Furthermore, many original members from all three churches were gone. Little has remained the same. This was no merger, transition, renewal or revival. It was a death and rebirth.

When I evaluate the problems some had with the merger, it seems their expectation was that we'd just add strategy, nomenclature, or staff to our "stellar" history and then—*poof*—we'd grow and become healthy. In some ways, we had swallowed the false concept of a magic pill. We thought we could tack on to our failing church culture a few principles from a book, cool ideas from a conference, or a sprinkling of proven effective formulas and—*voila*—we'd experience the cure! In fact, we had to die.

I realize that dying sounds harsh, but isn't it biblical? Do we not have to die to self in order to live for God? Yes, we do! As a church, we gave up our name, our leadership structure, our culture, even the names of certain rooms (see chapter 8 for examples). For all intents and purposes, Community Church died.

The death of Community Church made way for the birth of a new church, several new worship sites, and hundreds of new babes in Christ. Those not willing to make this sacrifice left. Those who stayed, received the blessing—more and more spiritual family members saved, sealed, and delivered for eternity. *They* became the crown and blessing (1 Thessalonians 2:19), not our European heritage or some other priority.

I honestly don't believe that our story is unique. At least our problems aren't. According to statisticians like Barna, Stetzer, and others, the modern church is little more than a super-sized version of Community Church. She's plateaued and is in decline.1 According to one study, The percentage of people attending church each weekend compared to overall population growth is in such decline that by 2050, the percentage of Americans attending church each weekend will be half of what it was in 1990.2 According to a recent *USA Toda* article, the number of people who call themselves "Christian" declined over 11% in the last generation.3 All of this brings us to this: The church is quickly becoming irrelevant in our society, an enigma to our culture. She is out of touch and powerless to meet the challenges of the world around her.

I used to marvel at how many longtime town residents had no idea that our 118-year-old church even existed. The average U.S. citizen is gleefully ignorant of the purpose or presence of the church. The Church has become a caricature of herself. She has her nice white buildings and stately columns, her organ music, robes, and other traditions—yet, she's almost completely disconnected from her community and the culture Jesus called her to reach. She looks the same as she did 100 years ago, but she's naïve and blind to the reality that nobody knows she exists. All of the needs citizens once had—education, food for the hungry, shelter for the homeless, care for the elderly, youth outreach, and more—are now handled by the government or a plethora of parachurch organizations. Who needs the church of Jesus Christ anyway?!

I believe all do—but not only are THEY ignorant of that fact, the church herself has forgotten it as well....

What is the solution?

In brief, I believe the solution is sacrifice—death and resurrection. It's seeking to lose our church life so that we might gain it. But in order to achieve that end, we must escape a false hope—it's what I call the facade of renewal!

Chapter 2

The Facade of Renewal

The church in America is dying. Nobody doubts it—foreign missionaries are being sent here to try and fix it. Attendance, offerings, doctrinal orthodoxy, ministry involvement, all the indicators of health are spiraling downward.4

Here in Connecticut, the home of one of the greatest revivals in history, our culture has now become an unreached people group, in missiological terms. Hartford, our capital city, is arguably the least evangelical city in the country. Yet, just a few miles north, in Enfield, Connecticut, Jonathan Edwards delivered his famous "Sinners in the Hands of an Angry God" sermon and set the world on fire.

We could naturally ask the question, "What happened?" In brief, we took our eyes off the ball. Post Edwards, churches in New England began to debate the legitimacy of the revival and divide over methodology instead of embracing the gospel and rejoicing in the impact of Edwards' ministry. The resulting division allowed the Enemy to establish strongholds that remain to this day. But while we could discuss and debate the history for years, I'd rather look forward and consider what we're doing about it.

Seeing her impending doom, we have seemingly decided to put the church on life support. We do this through denominational renewal programs, revival meetings, strategic planning sessions, transitioning seminars, etc. These tactical programs, at best, forestall the inevitable—but they don't truly present a cure. Symptoms may even disappear for a season, but still, her internal cancer grows.

You see, I would posit that all church transitioning/renewal programs fit neatly into one of two categories:

1. A short-term, external bandage attempt to cover up a terminal illness.
2. A misnamed ruse—a cover for the truth that the church must die in order to be reborn.

I would contend that option 2 is the only one that works, but I dislike the deception involved in its packaging (thus the blunt title of this book). Why option 2? Take a close look at the great revival stories of twentieth- and twenty-first-century churches. Most, like CC have lost many if not most of their original members, changed their names, remodeled or sold their original buildings, restructured or completely replaced their leadership, rewritten their vision and strategies, and more. The truth is, virtually *nothing* remains of their former selves. The original church died and something new has been born. The greatest example of this I know of is found in Dan Southerlands book, *Transitioning*. During it's "transition," Dan's church lost half its members, changed its name, restructured, reordered its worship and outreach strategies and ultimately moved into a new facility. Transition? I don't think so—I'd call it death and rebirth!5

Perhaps the reason many, if not most church renewals fail is that renewal is virtually impossible unless we're willing to die to self. I would also argue that the "successful renewals" have died and thus they are new church plants, not churches which have changed.

We Need a Spiritual AED

I took a first-aid certification class recently. One of our requirements was to learn to use an AED—an automatic electronic defibrillator. Now, most people assume that the Hollywood portrayal of AED usage is accurate, but nothing could be further from the truth. In the movies, the patient flat lines and the doctors try to jump-start his heart by shouting,

"Clear!" and then blasting him with a high voltage shock, using special coated paddles. If it works, the heart eventually restarts, assuming a normal, healthy rhythm.

Wrong!

AEDs don't start the heart. In fact, they actually *stop* the heart—momentarily killing the patient—so that his body will restart the heart with the correct rhythm. Typically, an AED isn't used when the patient has no pulse—it's used when a sporadic heartbeat is detected. If the irregular rhythm is allowed to continue, the heart will eventually become clogged with fluid, causing congestive heart failure and death. Thus, to prevent this, an electric shock stops the heart in the hopes that it will start anew and run in a healthy manner.

This is *exactly* what the modern church needs. She needs a spiritual AED. She needs to die—in order to live and be healthy.

"But Pastor Joel," you may be thinking, "we can't tell people that we're going to 'crucify' their beloved church! No church board or congregational committee will vote for *that*! Why can't we just call it a 'transition' or a 'revival' or a 'retooling exercise'? Wouldn't that be easier to swallow and thus be more effective?"

It amazes me that the same leaders who would "die on the hill" of ensuring an individual's conversion is truly based on repentance and the lordship of Christ, often fail to see that this applies to groups, i.e. churches! Do we "rightly handle the Word" by telling people to keep their old lifestyles and habits by just adding Jesus to everything "as is"? Acts 2:38 makes clear the biblical mandate to completely "turn" and go the other way. This mandate is true for individuals, why not for groups?

History bears out my premise here. Never has it been more efficient or effective to deceive into thinking renewal is good enough. Oh, it may look good at first, but eventually, the truth comes out that nothing has truly changed and the resulting conflict, hurt, and anger only make things worse. Could this be why studies show that most renewal efforts fail? Could this be why many pastors who try to slowly and patiently change their church's mission/vision, "go down in flames?" I could site more stats, but every pastor I know has a friend who tried to change things only to be shot out of the sky like a clay pigeon at a skeet range! Many of you reading this are probably still "licking the wounds" of your own attempts at transformation. You don't need statistics, you need solutions!

My experience has shown me that unless people accept and commit to total surrender (self-sacrifice), they won't grow. Again, what pastor would accept the conversion and membership of a person who says, "I want salvation as a free gift—but I don't want to surrender to the lordship of Christ. I just want to add Jesus to my life as-is and get my free fire insurance for the afterlife." Such a person would no doubt be told that repentance and true faith involve 100 percent commitment and surrender—carrying our cross, thus being crucified with Christ, so that we might live (Galatians 2:20).

So why *is* this same standard not applied to churches? Actually, I believe it is due to several mistaken assumptions:

- We assume that the majority of our members are saved. Based on the evident fruit (or more to the point, the lack of it) and Jesus' own prophecy regarding the lack of faith He'd find at His return, this is questionable. Jesus says "many" will be surprised to find that He "never knew" them (Matthew 7:23).
- We assume that just because our church members are saved, they will "default" to the Holy Spirit's guidance when it comes to the direction and focus of their local church. The fruit of history suggests that this is folly.
- We forget that true Christians are naturally peacemakers. Thus, when one or two "squeaky wheels" complain about a healthy, biblical mission, they can "win" since the majority will default to their position in order to maintain peace and avoid a split.
- We get overwhelmed by the task of trying to bring all of our members to the same point of change, like trying to get 100 clocks to chime at the same instant. It's tough! Seemingly impossible. Perhaps part of this is due to

the mistaken notion that all of our people really have to agree or be at the same point. We forget that the "big mo" of momentum is what's truly necessary for change, not 100% agreement.

- In some cases, we assume that our Western democratic church governance is biblical. Rightly or wrongly, the majority rules and thus, what they decide is God's will. Another version of this concept is a twisted view of the "priesthood of believers" where we think that the Holy Spirit will divinely guide the majority such that it will always reflect God's will.

How's this all working for us? Not so well.

The truth is—just like individual believers—churches must die. They have to carry their crosses so that they may live for Christ!

But who wants *that*? Most Christians, when faced with making the changes necessary to reach the lost and have a transformational impact on culture, run away or fight it to the death. Many pastors and theologians have even taken to extreme Reformed positions to justify inaction and make the status quo seem more righteous.

"After all," some argue, "the church isn't supposed to be 'missional;' it's supposed to be 'confessional.'" Having heard this argument personally, I'm really not sure what it means, other than that pastors don't want to engage culture "head-on," being "all things to all men that by all possible means I (we) might save some" (1 Corinthians 9:22). Instead they choose to make people in our culture approach them and attend 1950s-vintage worship services in order to be accepted by their increasingly irrelevant congregations.

In one church I pastored, one of the silliest battles I remember was over calling the foyer of the church building the "narthex" (old name) or the "lobby" (new name). When I first came to the church, people would mention "the narthex" and I honestly thought it was some kind of extinct bird on display in a back room somewhere. Eventually, I discovered that "the narthex" was the lobby in the front of our building. To his credit, in the interest of making the church more palatable and "homey" to visitors, one of our pastors began calling the narthex the "lobby." People freaked out! It was as if people were saying, "How dare he change the name of this sacred portion of the facility? Had he no shame?"

Clearly, people were unwilling to make even the simplest of changes to accommodate the unchurched and unsaved. In brief, they weren't willing to die to self.

My contention is that until we embrace the self-sacrifice necessary to change and grow, we will continue to see the evangelical church decline. If we don't die—we can't be reborn. It's that simple. It's also that biblical (as we'll see in the next chapter).

Chapter 3

A Biblical Foundation for Church Death and Rebirth

I tell you the truth, unless a kernel of wheat falls to the ground and dies, it remains only a single seed. But if it dies, it produces many seeds. The man who loves his life will lose it, while the man who hates his life in this world will keep it for eternal life. (John 12:24–25)

Jesus is clear here—the *only* way to produce fruit is to die and be regenerated with many seeds. I always think of evangelism here. I am to produce *many* fruit-producing seeds, not just nurture myself as one seed. But to do that, I must die. Is that not true of any church as well?

Give, and it will be given to you. A good measure, pressed down, shaken together and running over, will

be poured into your lap. For with the measure you use,
it will be measured to you. (Luke 6:38)

Most Christians don't believe this passage. Really! We believe that to give is to lose, not to gain. This is definitely true of many churches as well. If we give up something to reach the lost, we'll be hurt. If Luke 6:38 is true, we won't hurt and we won't lose. It says that if I try to out-give God, I'll lose (but that means I win, doesn't it?).

So when we sacrifice the organ to help a Christian rock band connect with unbelievers so they might hear the gospel and be saved, either God is a liar, or *we* will be blessed! If churches believed this, worship style wars and so many other sill battles would immediately cease.

Organ music is nowhere divinely ordained. And though contemporary music or instrumentation will not lead automatically to salvations, using culturally relevant musical styles removes a big hurdle for unsaved people. If they are engaged in worshiping Christ and thus drawn to Him for salvation—then let's do it! The only reason we won't is selfishness and the lack of a giving, generous spirit.

Therefore, if anyone is in Christ, he is a new creation;
the old has gone, the new has come! (2 Corinthians
5:17)

While I'm often critical of the conversion experiences of "believers" who have no fruit (see James 2:18), I think the biggest problem is that Christians are saved, yet ignorant of their true, new, identity in Christ. If I *truly* believed that I was a new creation, why on earth would I hold on to the past?

> I have been crucified with Christ and I no longer live, but Christ lives in me. The life I live in the body, I live by faith in the Son of God, who loved me and gave himself for me. (Galatians 2:20)

Here's the key—we live with and through Christ in us! If it's up to me, I'm toast! The good news is, I'm not living out the Christian life in my own strength. Neither is the body of Christ, the bride, Christ's church. If I remember that He gave Himself for me, what am I willing to give up for lost people I meet, or for my brothers and sisters in Christ who sit next to me in church?

> And anyone who does not take his cross and follow me is not worthy of me. Whoever finds his life will lose it, and whoever loses his life for my sake will find it. (Matt 10:38–39)

One of the ugly fruits of the modern "health and wealth 'gospel'" is that it focuses on getting material gain by becoming a Christian. This false gospel promises that if one becomes a believer, he'll be rich, healthy, successful, respected, and that life will be beautiful all the time. It collapses on itself, for it cannot be reconciled with the true gospel to which persecuted Christians in places like China and Sudan cling—even at the risk of their lives. Is the true gospel worth the sacrifice of self? Are peace of mind and a clean conscience worth the sacrifice of self? Oh, yes; *eternally* worth it!

So why is it that churches can't even give up a denominational name that confuses or scares non-Christians? Why can't they give up ties, or robes, or the "King James only" mindset?

But someone may ask, "How are the dead raised? With what kind of body will they come?" How foolish! What you sow does not come to life unless it dies. When you sow, you do not plant the body that will be, but just a seed, perhaps of wheat or of something else. But God gives it a body as he has determined, and to each kind of seed he gives its own body. (1 Corinthians 15:35–38)

When we are resurrected, this old body is *not* the one we get back (Can I get an amen? Glory, Hallelujah!). So why is it that when we rebirth a church, we want the old everything? Can we not trust God to give us something better?

> What shall we say, then? Shall we go on sinning so that grace may increase? By no means! We died to sin; how can we live in it any longer? Or don't you know that all of us who were baptized into Christ Jesus were baptized into his death? We were therefore buried with him through baptism into death in order that, just as Christ was raised from the dead through the glory of the Father, we too may live a new life. (Romans 6:1–4)

When we grasp the power of this passage, our lives and the collective life of the church will change forever! We *truly* are dead to sin. It's gone. We now have the power to reject and walk away from it. We don't have to walk in drunkenness, sexual sin, selfish ignorance of our unchurched neighbors. We don't need to come to virtual blows in our church business meetings anymore—that is dead. Or at least it can be. We can really live a new life!

Every pastor, elder, deacon, or ministry leader worth his or her salt would passionately agree that without a total surrender and dedication to the truth of Romans 6:1-4, a person cannot be saved, let alone live a godly, sanctified life! While we may interpret the verses differently, the bottom line is the same—personal salvation and total surrender to the lordship of Christ are inextricably connected, if not synonymous.

But what about churches?

While I'll save my ecclesiology for a later chapter, I would suggest that every evangelical leader knows that the church is a collective group, set apart or called out by God. In other words, what in principle applies to individuals will inevitably be carried over to churches since the church is the sum total of those individuals.

The church *is* people. It's not a building, corporation, denomination, or set of programs. The church is a group of saved, called-out believers, established in the truths taught by Christ and the apostles, inclusive of the five primary purposes of God, Worship, Evangelism, Ministry, Discipleship, and Fellowship), and entrusted to elders who meet the criteria of 1 Timothy 3 and Titus 1.

We see this in what are commonly called the "household texts." Throughout his epistles, Paul makes an unquestionable parallel between the household of a typical church family and the "household of God," or church. Why? Because the church is a group of households and households are made up of individuals. So, if a church is people and those people have to die to self in order to live, doesn't the established church need to be reestablished through death and rebirth as well?

Some would argue at this point that *if* all the individuals in the church had truly died to self, the church would already be dead to self. On the one hand, I agree, but it's a moot point. Every pastor knows that most churches are composed of a mixture of "sheep and goats." Some truly have been saved, but others, not so much. It is the latter who will often still oppose the things of God because they aren't truly dead to self.

Furthermore, even *if* they are all saved, and thus dead to self, there are collective, communal lessons to learn and commitments to make. Individual believers have to pick up their crosses and follow Jesus, but that's a daily challenge. It is for churches as well. And, if the church carries its cross and follows Jesus, isn't it true that at any moment she may be asked to drive that crucifix into the ground and climb on?

You bet!

So most of what applies to individuals, applies to the collective body of Christ:

- She must carry her cross daily, remembering that she is dead to self, but alive in Christ.
- She must know that she exists only through and for Christ.
- She must constantly die to the old and give birth to the new.
- She must give and thus be blessed.

- She must continually lose her life to find true life.
- She must participate in the death, burial, and resurrection of Jesus—thus receiving a new church life, not just a warmed-over, old congregation.
- She must have and embrace a new identity in Christ.

What does this look like?

In many ways, it's invisible. It's an internal commitment to do and become anything in order to obey and follow Jesus. Most commonly, it springs into action and thus becomes visible when a challenge is presented. That challenge could be to reach a new people group taking root in the community. For example, in retrospect, I'm convinced that the decline of many modern churches actually started in the 1960s when so many Caucasians fled the inner city and its ethnic changes to take refuge in the suburbs.

WWJD (What Would Jesus Do)? Jesus would have stayed and reached out to African American families, Hispanic families, and families of all other races, as they came into the neighborhood. The church would have reflected the diversity of the community around her. Instead, she withdrew to a "safe" place based on her own comfort and desire.

The internal commitment to change would result in external action to do whatever is necessary to reach a lost, confused, and dying younger generation with the gospel. While this change should never involve surrendering the message of the gospel, it almost *always* means sacrificing some methods we use to share it.

In my experience, here are several common methods or characteristics we change when we seek to reach outside the church and thus impact our community for Christ. Some of these will be addressed in more depth later, but here's a quick summary:

- **Music.** I hate the phrase "worship wars" because it is a screamingly ironic oxymoron. Still, we have them. Why? Selfishness—plain and simple. I like what I like and I don't care what you like. Period! But what if we all unselfishly asked, "What does our lost community like in terms of musical style?" and "What if we tried to use music as a vehicle to drive the gospel *to* people who wouldn't hear it otherwise?" We must answer these questions honestly and sacrifice old style(s) that do not pass the "test" of the answers that mandate change.

  While it's true that worship is about expressing love to God more than it is a marketing tool to reach people, the question must always be, "What style and instrumentation will help our community praise Him, draw them to Him, open them up to accept the gospel, and be transformed?"

What I personally like as a worship style is irrelevant. What's relevant is what will accomplish the mission of Matthew 28:19–20, to make disciples of all peoples! The result of selfishness driving the internal church battles over this subject has left the church ten to twenty years behind our culture and thus, unable to reach it. For example, while we're still fighting the "contemporary versus traditional" war, millennial generation youth have decided to pursue what some call "ancient modern" liturgy. Thus, about the time some of our churches have finally decided to break down and allow a few praise choruses, many of our thirty-and-under seekers are no longer interested in contemporary worship forms. Way to go church! Selflessness would allow us to be "lean and mean," able to adapt methods *much* more quickly to reach a lost and dying world.

- **Dress.** I remember when this "came to a head" at our church. I made the mistake of leaving my tie in the closet for a few weeks and was approached by our deaconesses who made sure I knew that I looked "much more handsome with a tie on." While subtle, the point became more blatant as time went on.

At the same time, more and more teens were coming to services wearing jeans and T-shirts, my daughter amongst them. The contrast between the dress of our youth and the formal dress of our seniors became more glaring over time. One day, I asked my daughter about it. I told her that many of the folks at church dressed up to show respect for God. With humility and gentleness, she looked me in the eye and asked, "Daddy, if I dress up to go to church, who would I really be doing it for and who would I really be trying to impress? Would it be God, who knows my style and dress every day, and loves me the way He made me? Or would it be Mrs. So-and-so at church?" That was it—the dress code issue was settled in my psyche once and for all.

The *only* concern I have now is for those we're trying to reach. I ask myself, "If I wear this, will the visitors feel comfortable?" Beyond that, I don't care what anyone wears as long as it's modest.

- **Seating.** Most churches find chairs work better than pews. Yet pews are traditional and thus considered sacred. I've seen people battle over shellac versus paint for the pews—let alone the question of removing them! In our church, the argument would be sitting at Starbucks-like tables versus chairs, set theater-style. We have both, but I've told the church plainly, if one helps us reach the lost and the other doesn't; the one that doesn't help us goes!

This is a good place to address a related issue. *Why do we do "seeker-sensitive" things? Is it to appease or mimic culture?* On the other hand, if we keep pews, organs, and hymns—is it to appease our members? Neither motive is good. Some argue that certain forms of worship and certain seating arrangements better honor or glorify God. Really? So, God likes Bach and pews, eh? I'll bet he's a Republican, too, right? Wrong! We *should* do everything to honor God (2 Corinthians 4:15).

We honor God the most by obeying His call to make disciples of all nations, of all people groups (Matthew 28:19). So, if my style of worship and my seating arrangements *help* people forget their self-conscious worry about fitting in, and the music feels familiar, allowing them to focus *completely* on Jesus, I'm honoring God—in total obedience. If not, I'm in selfish sin—plain and simple!

- **Language and Bible Translations.** Will we use what I call "twenty-five-cent theological terms" or will we speak plainly and clearly for folks who are unchurched? Will I read the KJV translation because "King James English was good enough for Jesus and is thus good enough for me," as one person ignorantly put it. Most churches have to move to a modern translation and language that's "visitor-friendly."

I remember one of our churches would invite members to share prayer requests during our services. It seemed people would always ask for "traveling mercies" for themselves or others. I had no idea what that meant, and I was the pastor. I used to think it was those Boy Scout rest stop services where they give out free coffee and donuts. I learned that it meant prayers for protection as we drive. Why should someone have to learn a new language to go to church?

- **Meeting Schedules.** Times and places of meetings sometimes have to be adjusted to consider new people. We used to have a Sunday night service. It became the internal measurement of who was really spiritually "with it" and who was clearly spiritually immature. In fact, over time, it had dwindled simply because most families had work or school early Monday morning and couldn't justify being at church all morning and then coming back in the evening. If this was true for members, how much more for non-members. It was time to have a different venue for gospel presentations and outreach.

- **Discipleship Formats.** This is usually a change from Sunday school or Bible studies to small groups and the like. Rarely does biblical principle enter this debate, or even basic human logic. It's simply an emotional attachment to the idea. "I was saved in Sunday School," some reason, "so how could we *ever* get rid of it?" The concept of doing it in home groups, one-on-one via mentoring, and others are often not even seriously considered, or if they are, there's a battle.

- **Budget.** Oh, now I *have* "quit preachin' and gone to meddlin!" You can tell people, as I have, that everything they've believed for fifty years is biblically bogus, that they belong to a cult, that you're going to do away with everything from styles of music to missions committees—but don't you *dare* mess with the budget! It's a death sentence for many pastors. Most churches don't have evangelism budgets. Adding one and transferring dollars from other line items is a challenge.

- **Ministries.** "Sacred cow" ministries often must become barbeques in order to free people to start new ministries designed to reach or meet needs in the community. This is hard, but fruitful, when done right. A "sacred cow" ministry is a ministry that's untouchable and can never be modified or eliminated no matter how effective or ineffective it may be. The term comes from India where, for Hindus, cows are considered sacred and thus never killed as a food source—even for starving people.

In churches, sacred cows can take several forms. For example, in one church I pastored, one person we supported from our missions budget was a family member of the missions chairman. Obviously, when financial cuts were considered, that line item was understood to be a "sacred cow."

- **Missions.** A paradigm shift that sees missions as church planting and multiplication, nothing more and nothing less, is a must for church health. To most established churches, any money spent on anything outside their own congregation is a "mission." For example, one of our churches supported people who taught Sunday school in established churches in other countries. A nice ministry, but not necessarily a biblical mission. This had to change so money could be spent on winning souls and starting new churches.
- **Structure/Polity.** Rarely can the inherent selfishness protected by congregational democracy be biblically productive. Leaders must lead. Members must do ministry, not maintenance, as Rick Warren has so effectively taught.

49

I'm sure there are more, but these stand out. The bottom line is that *no* church can survive these kinds of dramatic, often traumatic changes. That's precisely why she must die and be resurrected anew. I believe a close study of 1 Corinthians 15 and the case studies of most "successful" church renewals proves that when a church "transition," "turn-around," or "renewal" works, "the old has passed away and the new has come."

This is precisely why these "transformed" churches often have:

- A new name.
- A new leadership team.
- A new building or a renovated old building.
- New logo and decor.
- New vision and mission statement.
- New structure (normally staff and/or elder-led, instead of congregational).
- A new budget (purpose-driven versus rigid and unbending).

And, not surprisingly,

- New members. Most often, the majority of original members leave, new folks are saved and quickly become involved, producing a new majority—a dominant force of new sheep in the newborn flock.

In other words, even if we're in denial about it, we have a new church!

Chapter 4

Crucifying Your Church Doctrinally

I held off on this topic purposefully, in the hope that you'd be "with me" regarding the basic premise of church death and rebirth. If you are, this chapter will make sense and just add "fuel to the fire." If you're not, I pray that this chapter will change your mind.

I believe the Church in America needs a doctrinal over-haul. There are some key truths of scripture that we've either, tossed-out, watered down, or just ignored for far too long. And, while I stand by everything written in chapter 3, the following doctrinal corrections actually must be made *before* a church can be reborn.

The Breadth of the Gospel

Far more than the summary found in the kerygma or "proclamation" used by the early church fathers, the gospel is everything Jesus is, was, taught, lived, did, and will do in the future. This is a *huge* concept, far bigger than the popular "four points and a prayer" tip of the gospel iceberg.

Paul wrote, "For I am not ashamed of the gospel, because it is the power of God for the salvation of everyone who believes: first for the Jew, then for the Gentile" (Romans 1:16).

But which gospel?

Was this powerful, salvation producing gospel, the classic version presented at most tent meetings or evangelistic crusades? Was it a good-news-only gospel? Maybe it was the gospel of social justice and provision so prevalent in postmodern circles. Perhaps it is the gospel of baptism of the Spirit with the evidence of speaking in tongues as our Pentecostal friends assert.

While mine may be the less popular view, I would argue that the gospel Jesus, Paul, and the other apostles preached was the gospel of the Kingdom of God referenced in Matthew 4:23, 9:25, 24:14, and elsewhere. It includes all of the elements described above and more. For example, notice Matthew 4:23 (KJV):

And Jesus went about all Galilee, teaching in their synagogues, and preaching the gospel of the kingdom, and healing all manner of sickness and all manner of disease among the people.

Matthew seems to connect the verbal teaching of the kingdom with healing. Also, his use of the phrase "gospel of the kingdom" seems to include all kingdom elements (leadership, location/territory, subjects, and covenant/law). It's not just a reference to his death and resurrection, although it no doubt includes these critical elements. Also, notice Peter's sermon in Acts 10. Peter includes fulfilled prophesy, Jesus' teaching about morality, and the existence of spiritual gifts, all as part of his message. This goes far beyond the "Four Spiritual Laws," "Romans Road," or other evangelical gospel presentations.

This gospel is complete, rich, and all-encompassing. The gospel is everything Jesus taught and everything Jesus is. It cannot be shared in thirty seconds by reading bullet points off an index card, nor should we attempt this necessarily. Rather, when we return to our roots and evaluate Peter's early sermons in Acts 2, Acts 10, and elsewhere, we see two things:

1. Most of the recipients of these messages already had a deep understanding of Old Testament scriptures

including types, prophecies, and the law. We know this because they were either Jews who had studied (and often memorized) major portions of the Torah or they were Gentile proselytes (God-fearers) who had been exposed to the same. Many times, the book of Acts tells us that Paul and others specifically sought-out "God-fearers" to start new churches. Thus, when we see their sermons in print, we must assume the audience includes primarily these people.

2. What the apostles presented as the gospel was much broader and richer than what we present as "the gospel" today, as we've demonstrated above.

One thing's for sure: when we compare what the Jews on Pentecost in 33 A.D. knew versus what the average "Evangelism Crusade" attendee knows today. There is a massive difference. What folks know today before making a decision for Christ is a small fraction of what the first century Christians knew. Even if we argue about what components are necessary as part of the gospel, we cannot argue about the discrepancy of knowledge. How do we know that even Gentiles knew more than the average unchurched American today?

First, most were God-fearers who had been worshiping in the outer courts of Jewish temples for years.

Consider the scene at Pentecost, circa 33 AD (see Acts 2). These people had traveled for days or weeks just to celebrate a Jewish festival. We can't even get most Americans out of bed for a 10 a.m. service, five minutes from their home! Second, the content of the message given by the apostles was much richer than our modern four points and a prayer.

God fearing Gentiles and Jews would have kept the 7 annual Jewish festivals. These festivals included rich symbolism, demonstrated through Passover, Unleavened Bread, Pentecost, Atonement, Trumpets, The Feast of Tabernacles, and the Last Great Day of Tabernacles (Leviticus 23). Most scholars agree that these point to the sacrifice of Jesus, sanctification, the birth of the Church, the future banishing of Satan, the return of Christ, and the eternal kingdom of God being established, and the new heavens and earth, respectively. Living out and understanding these shadows (Colossians 2:17) helped set the stage for the gospel in all its fullness. Most Christians (let alone non-Christians) are ignorant of these foundational truths.

So, we know that early Christians were taught more, prior to salvation. We also know that there is a vast difference between the gospel preached in the first century and the gospel messages shared by various twenty-first century Christian groups.

But does it matter? When we consider the sad state of the modern church, I believe the answer is a resounding, *"Yes!"*

The gospel is the power of God (Romans 1:16) and our modern churches are weak and dying. Estimates now indicate that over eighty percent of evangelical churches are plateaued or in decline.6 We're missing the gospel! Where there is no power, there is no gospel—period!

And let's not forget that the gospel is the power of God unto salvation—so the lack of evangelism, growth, and continued health all hinge on this point (Romans 1:16):

✓ Evangelicals have the kerygma summary of 1 Corinthians 1:23, but are dying.
✓ Charismatics have the "full gospel" Holy Spirit gifting, but are closing churches daily across the U.S.7
✓ Emergent churches understand the social gospel of service, but lack true conversion growth, repentance, and fruit.8

✓ Mainline denominations have abandoned all of the above and are the most rapidly declining group among us. 9

Maybe—just maybe, the fragmented, summarized, depleted message is the real problem.

So what is the gospel?

1. **The gospel is everything Jesus taught.** It's referred to as the gospel of the Kingdom in scripture, and kingdoms are by definition, multifaceted. We glibly refer to the first four books in the New Testament as "the gospels," but then quickly edit them down to virtual sound bites. The gospel of the Kingdom includes our state as sinners, Jesus' virgin birth, His sinless life, His suffering and death on the cross, His resurrection, our faith as the means of salvation, and His return with our reward, but it includes much more as well.

2. **The gospel must include social justice.** It includes everything Jesus did. He healed the sick and fed the hungry as He preached. We cannot separate these actions from the gospel itself—they *are* the gospel—the good news of Jesus.

3. **The gospel is everything Jesus is, was, and will be.** Jesus *is* the gospel, so His humanity and divinity are

both part of the equation. Jesus set an example, so to live out the gospel, we explore and become students of Jesus' identity in order to grow. The gospels are the greatest source of this understanding. What did Jesus do? Where did he spend his time? What were His priorities? What did he refer to from the past and history? What are his promises for the future? The gospel is *all* Jesus said, not just what He did on the cross and when He rose from the dead. His death and resurrection are two pillars of faith, for sure, but to reduce the gospel to these two events ignores over three years of powerful teaching and His daily real-life example—let alone centuries of prophetic teaching about the person of Christ.

How should we fix this?

I think we must first stop assuming that people have a basic understanding of biblical truths, or what Chuck Colson and others refer to as a *biblical worldview*. When Paul went to a new city, the first thing he would do is find Jews who knew the scriptures. Next, he'd seek out God-fearers and preach to them. Why? They understood the Old Testament and would more readily recognize and receive Jesus' role as Savior and Lord. People without that foundation would not. Unfortunately, we live in a culture that does *not* have this foundation, but we preach to them and act as if they do.

For example, we teach people to evangelize by quoting a few verses in Romans (the "Romans Road"). We tell them all are sinners (Romans 3:23), that the wages of sin is death (Romans 6:23a), but that the gift of God is eternal life in Christ Jesus (Romans 6:23b), and so forth. That's great, except we might as well be quoting from *Readers Digest* since these folks don't believe the Bible is true, inspired, and thus authoritative at all. Then we give them an invitation to pray a quick prayer and be guaranteed a joy-filled eternity.

Some say "Yes," just to get us off their backs (like a lady who buys the stupid vacuum cleaner just to get rid of the pesky salesman). Others believe the short, "Cliffs Notes" version and pray the prayer because, well, "who wouldn't?" If I told you I'd give you a million dollars, with no strings attached, *if* you would simply repeat a short paragraph after me—wouldn't *you*?

People need to know the Bible is reliable. They need to know there is a God. Then (and only then), they need to hear the whole gospel. New Tribes Missions tells the entire story of the Bible to unreached people *before* they make an evangelistic invitation. Sure it takes time, but it works! My favorite missionary video of all time is *Ee-Taow!* It is the story of a New Guinean tribe accepting Jesus en masse. If you watch it, you'll understand exactly the importance of sharing the whole gospel. 10

The Link between Discipleship and Evangelism

Philemon 1:6 tells us that we won't understand all the good things we have in Christ until we're actively sharing our faith. Jesus said that being a disciple was synonymous with fishing for men (Matthew 4:19). Our churches cannot grow until people realize that being a disciple is a lot more than just reading the Bible and learning stuff! In our church, we use the acrostic "T.E.A.C.H." as a tool for understanding this process:

T = Transfer information. We need the truth. It must be shared in classes, sermons, in books, and brochures, and more. Still, this is just the beginning and most churches stop here.

E = Embody. The truth must be modeled by those mentored to do that modeling. Most leaders haven't had mentors, so it is no wonder they don't provide mentoring for new believers.

A = Apply. The student disciple must apply what is shared and modeled. So, when we teach on evangelism, the student must do it, or we haven't discipled him. Further, if being a disciple is equal to being a "fisher of men," the student isn't even a true disciple of Christ until he shares his faith.

C = Critique. The mentor must give feedback on the performance of the student. This allows for improvement and growth.

H = Hand off. This is almost never done! I would argue that the disciple isn't mature and thus he doesn't "graduate" as a true disciple, versus an apprentice, until he shares the same training with another student. Again, he or she must be a "fisher of men."

So, sharing the gospel is part and parcel with being a disciple. Churches that allow people to be members, though they never share their faith, are living a lie. Anyone who doesn't "fish" for men, has no business calling himself a disciple. And, if a person isn't a true follower/disciple of Jesus, he has no business being a member of a biblical church.

The Inseparable Unity of Service and Evangelism

Everywhere Jesus went, he consistently served and shared the gospel. He *never* separated the gospel message from feeding and caring for others. In other words, healing the sick and feeding the hungry were *always* accompanied by preaching the good news…and vice versa.

Lest someone argue from silence to suggest that preaching without healing or feeding occurred, the very nature of Christ and his testimony proves that the Apostles only normative experience was that Jesus healed and fed people *everywhere* they went (see Matthew 4:23). To suggest that preaching occurred without accompanying actions of social justice *just* because they aren't always mentioned, calls into question the narrative and normative experience outlined by the gospel authors. Today, it's popular to do one over the other.

Why do we separate them? I think its vanity. We like to distinguish ourselves from other churches or denominations and movements. "We're not like *those* people who _____" (fill in the blank). If we see people who do more preaching than feeding, we feed and brag. If we see people who do more feeding, we preach and brag. The extremes are contrasts built on pride.

We must make a diligent effort to preach the gospel, along with feeding, serving and helping—always. Never should we hide what we believe or be ashamed to speak up about Jesus. At the same time, how can we represent Him if we just preach

63

to people, but never help them with physical needs? Isn't that a misrepresentation of who He really is?

Missions as Church Planting/Multiplication

Nowhere did the apostles win souls, build a school or plant a garden for hungry people without starting a church so that the people could continue to be fed. In fact, the historical records we have (the Acts and Pauline Epistles primarily), describe *only* the creation of churches. I'm not suggesting that these other things could not have been done. I *am* suggesting that the Biblical record nowhere suggests that they were the priority, or that they were ever done apart from church planting and establishment.

From the time of Antioch in Acts 13, the model has been clear—missions *is* planting, nothing more and nothing less. We can argue that missions involves other cultures, but we cannot biblically argue that it involves things separate from church planting.

What's sad today is that the definition of missions has been corrupted.

At Community Church, we gave 25% percent of our budget to what we called "missions." Sadly, however, virtually none of this went to church planting. Instead, we supported everything from non-evangelistic Christian radio programming, to people who taught music to college students, to folks teaching Sunday School classes on foreign soil.

So we said we were all about missions, yet we did things that weren't truly missional because they were divorced from church planting.

Part of this doctrinal dichotomy comes from a flawed ecclesiology. Our view of the church is warped. Unless we understand that the local church is the epicenter and focus of God's work on earth, the missiology I've described above won't make sense. You see, the modern church has given away most of her identity and responsibility to the government and to parachurch organizations. Thus, she's become a shadow of herself—a caricature of what she once was. This is why so many churches are viewed as irrelevant in our culture, especially to most people under thirty.

Here's just a partial list of things the church used to do in society, but rarely does anymore:

- **Care for the poor and homeless.** From the first century on, it was the church that cared for the poor, setting aside special "widow funds," soup kitchens and other programs for those in need. But today, we call on the United Way or the Welfare system.
- **Counseling the depressed, hurting, or mentally challenged.** Even "Christian Counseling" has turned

pseudo-secular. Guiding people using Scripture is considered passé, if not dangerous. In response, pastors refer to outside counselors as an almost knee-jerk reaction to the expression of a felt need. (I should mention that my wife is a School Psychologist. Also, we have a Director of Pastoral Care on my staff who is a licensed Clinical Social Worker and Therapist. I'm not opposed to counseling—I just oppose Churches handing it off instead of owning their call to heal the brokenhearted!

- **Reaching out to college students or high school kids in trouble.** We used to do this, but now we call on state run youth programs, the government's Department of Children and Families, (DCF), or parachurch college ministries.

- **Serving the needs of the elderly.** Why can't we visit them, care for them in their homes, help feed them, assist with lawn care, etc.? Instead, we leave that to local governments. It wasn't always that way!

- **Holding forums/debates on political or social issues in the community.** As I type this, I'm in Arlington, VT. Not far from here, in Bennington, VT, there stands an old congregational church where the VT constitution was penned and debates were held re. Vermont's cooperation with the other 12 colonies in the original

US constitution. Today, that debate wouldn't even be allowed in church.

- **Serving the unique needs of men.** Our churches used to be places where men could go to find friendship and an "iron sharpens iron" environment. Churches have largely been feminized, such that many men don't even feel comfortable in worship services. The music is soft and emotional, the seating is close and "cozy," and the ministries lend themselves to verbal connection. Most guys want just the opposite of all of this. So, we've given-over the ministry to groups like Promise Keepers and others.

- **Education.** To demonstrate how far we've come in this category, I'd simply point out that most Christians are ignorant of the fact that the entire western university system was birthed by, in, for and through—you guessed it—the Church! Further, as settlers explored the west, it was often local pastors and churches which ran the only schools and taught people to read using the Bible. Today, we sometimes look down on people or churches considering a church-based education program. Why? Do we really think our government is doing a better job?

- **Serving the unique needs of women.** While the church has a soft, feminine worship climate, the presence of men and the absence of sound women's groups has led to a need for "Women of Faith" conferences and other programs. Again, I'm not against these—I'm just against the idea that local churches defer their responsibilities to these outside programs.

With these items being handled by Uncle Sam, groups like Promise Keepers, parachurch groups like Campus Crusade, secular counselors, or whoever, is it any wonder churches aren't more important in our culture? And, is it any wonder that we think of "missions" as doing almost anything *but* planting a church?

Church and Competency-Based Theological Education

Over the centuries, the church has slowly turned inward and thus abdicated her roles and responsibilities as described above. Still, there is perhaps no greater example of abdication than the creation of a whole new genre of institutions called seminaries. If church leaders identified, mentored, taught, and commissioned leaders as Paul and other first-century leaders did, what role would seminaries play? Would they even be necessary? Think about it:

- **Churches provide local experience and mentor-based training.** Seminaries provide classroom-oriented information transfer. Which of these best reflects the way of Christ with his disciples and the way of the apostles? Which better prepares students to be disciples and thus, leaders?

- **Churches are the focal point of God's ministry on the planet.** Students in the church are doing ministry as they learn. Students in seminaries are placed in manmade creations that are, though rich with resources churches often lack, unable to offer a real world environment.

- **Churches aren't expensive to attend.** Seminaries, on the other hand, often cost $25,000 or more per year.

What if seminaries began to see themselves as resource centers for church-based training? What would change? What would stay the same? How would the church become more productive?

In the interest of honesty and full disclosure, I have been to seminary. I have an undergraduate degree in theology and master's degrees in both religion and religious education from Liberty University in Virginia. I'd be a hypocrite if I said I oppose seminaries altogether. Still, I question their genesis and wonder how much better our modern evangelical world would be if churches maintained responsibility for training leaders, including pastors.

I also wonder what it would look like if mentoring relationships required, as in rabbinic circles, the mastery of certain ministerial competencies prior to commissioning. That is, what if pastors had to *do* ministry in order to be credentialed in ministry? Isn't this the essence of 1 Timothy 3, Titus 1, and other passages? Where did we get the idea that, if a guy gets enough right answers on the multiple-choice exams of seminary, and writes a few good papers, he's qualified to lead a church?

On this subject, I would strongly recommend the reader look closely at BILD International and the Antioch School of church planting and leadership development in Ames, Iowa. Paradigm papers and a whole host of other material are available at www.bild.org. The newly accredited Antioch program stands on two pillars which, I believe are the keys to the future of the church.

First, they promote church-based theological education. Our churches are filled with young people who should be prepared for ministry. Instead, only a few who seek it are sent away to seminary, never to return. Why not have training that is fully in, by, and for the local church? This is *not* distance education, but rather leadership development as part of the body and life of every local church.

The second pillar is competency-based education. This means that degrees are granted based on a portfolio of accomplishments, not on multiple-choice exams and the like. In the Antioch program, there are no tests and everybody gets a pass or fail grade based on an electronic portfolio of ministry experiences, much like an artist's portfolio of work would be used to grant his or her degree.

What if every one of our 450,000+ churches began to produce new leaders and pastors? What would happen to our impact on our world? How would this impact the health of our churches? How would ministries in our churches grow? How many new churches would be birthed? Can you see it? A truly amazing vision, isn't it?

The Role of Elders in the Church

Even a quick read of the New Testament makes it clear that having elders—and knowing why—is a must to church health. (See appendix ii, "Just What IS an Elder Anyway?"). An elder is an overseer, a spiritual leader. His job is to make decisions and teach. Without elders, we have mob rule at best and unbridled heresy at worst in our churches. Paul repeatedly instructed his apprentices to "ordain elders in every city" (Titus 1:5). Perhaps God and Paul knew what they were doing! Why Elders?

Every organization needs competent, called, and qualified leadership. Ironically, the church in America has become more democratic than even our secular political system. That is, we see democracy and voting as essential to our nature whereas our nation understands that voting is used to empower leaders, not to make every decision, minor or major, en masse.

Historians agree that our nation is, from its founding, a representative republic, not a true democracy. We elect representatives who lead us. Yet, in most churches, we vote on everything from toilet paper to the doctrine of the Trinity. Worse yet, the guy who got saved and became a member last week has just as much authority and voting clout as the senior pastor.

Can you imagine a corporation like Xerox running this way? They'd be out of business in a week! What if sports teams ran this way? Imagine the UCONN Huskies women's basketball team voting on every play. By the time they decided who would bring the ball down the court, the other team would have already scored. It's ridiculous, yet "normal," to many churches.

Every team has a captain and each player has a position. Wisdom and Scripture indicate that the church needs elders and ministry team players instead of what I call "mob rule" democracy. Much more could be said on this, but suffice it to say that without the role of elders clarified and implemented biblically, no church will reach her true potential.

Hell, Satan, Demons, and Spiritual Warfare

If we endeavor to rebirth a church, we will encounter Satan head-on. One preacher said, "If you *don't* run into the devil, you're running in the wrong direction!" Since 59 percent of all Americans think that the devil is only a metaphor, we've got our work cut out for us!11 It's not popular or politically correct for western Christians, especially evangelicals, to talk about literal encounters with demons, but my experience in planting is that we must.

When Paul says, in Ephesians 6, that our battle is not against flesh and blood, he makes it clear that, whether we know it or not, we're at war. Churches need to believe this and take action to deal with it. While many great tools exist to disciple people through this topic and implement a strategy for spiritual warfare, the method is less important than the message and the message here is to watch and fight.

Then we have the ever-present battle about the reality of hell. How is it that Catholic Christians can embrace the idea that the Eucharist literally changes to become the actual flesh of Jesus, and many mainline church leaders believe it at least embraces the presence of Jesus in a supernatural way (transubstantiation or consubstantiation), yet, when we talk about demons or the literal reality of hell, so many of these same folks shrug in disbelief?

Jesus talked about hell as a literal location more than any other New Testament teacher. Furthermore, Jesus repeatedly encountered demons and told His disciples that they would as well. Why do we believe this has changed?

Worship as the Fuel of Ministry

Too often, churches think of worship as simple entertainment. It's just the music we either like or hate (and thus like to complain about). Worship is far more than simply music. When worship is expressed musically, it is light-years beyond entertainment.

Individually, worship is prayer, Bible study, meditation, and fasting at times; all to express love for God and to draw closer to Him. A church can't grow without collective commitment to these same things. Thanks to Rick Warren, we understand our call to evangelism, fellowship, discipleship, ministry, and so on. But I would argue that without worship, the power to accomplish these is absent.

Love Versus Liberalism or Legalism

Why do we think we're so much smarter than God? Most evangelicals believe that God inspired the Bible and that it is "without error in its original manuscripts." Yet, we add to it and take away from it all the time.

For example, Fundamentalists are willing to die to uphold the inerrancy of scripture and they live for *sola scriptura* debates over the question of the Bible's sufficiency in all matters of faith and practice. Yet, even though Jesus' first miracle was turning water into wine, they'll condemn anyone who drinks a glass. I used to joke that Jesus' first miracle was turning water into wine and the Baptist's first miracle was changing it into grape juice. We all know it wasn't juice, and we know the biblical command is against drunkenness, not against having a glass of wine, so why "play games" by adding to the scriptural requirements?

On the other hand, our liberal friends like to play what I call, "doctrinal smorgasbord" with Scripture. The joy of smorgasbords is to take what you like, a little here, a little there, and leave what you don't like at the buffet. They like passages about God's love, but those "distasteful wrath verses" aren't read too often. They like "inclusive" language, but anything seemingly intolerant is ignored.

I attended a funeral service recently, conducted by a liberal pastor in our area. As he read a list of comforting verses to the grieving family, he came to John 14:6. I know him personally, and know that he is a proponent of liberal ecumenical thought. So, when he came to the part where Jesus says, "No one comes to the Father except through me," he just skipped it and went to the next verse. How dare we pick and choose from God's Word?

Why can't we just focus on what *is* in scripture without adding to it or taking away from it? There's plenty to talk about and, I believe, sufficient truth to transform us, without editing. It comforts at times and convicts as well. For example, love is a *great* comfort. Yet, the great commandments are also *more* than indicting for most of us.

For instance, I may not steal from my brother, but have I truly loved him if I won't give him a hot meal when he's hungry? Furthermore, I may claim to love my brother because I have warm feelings for his plight, but if my tolerant view of his lifestyle enables behavior that will lead to spiritual or physical destruction—is that *truly* love?

Most churches need to take a close look at what I call their "unwritten" statement of faith. The written one is probably fine (although in some cases it needs work too), but it's often the *unwritten* or *understood* statement that is a mess. This takes brutal honesty and a willingness to confess sin and move forward in repentant change. I believe that churches that will do this are always blessed. Those who refuse to do so will *not* hear Jesus say, "Well done" at His return.

For example, if you know that your unwritten statement of faith says that it's a sin to go to a bar, yet you know that reaching-out to people in that environment is a major opportunity to connect with lost people, you may need to address this openly and publicly. It's not a sin to go to a bar and reach out to the lost. In fact, it's exactly what Jesus would do and, in the cultural context of His day, it's what he *DID*!

Perhaps this is a good place to talk about love over legalism in the process of church death and rebirth. Is it loving to crucify a church? Is it loving to let go of older members who can't adjust to the changes you're making? How do we proceed through this in a biblically loving way?

First, let's remember that God is love and yet, he corrects and even gets angry with his children sometimes. Love includes what we sometimes call "tough love" too. I have two children who are now young adults. While they were growing up, to love them sometimes meant I had to punish or correct them. Loving them sometimes meant I had to say, "No!" I've known parents who had to remove an older child from their home because of his/her destructive behavior. Often, my pastoral duty was to comfort them with the assurance that this act was a loving act because it might produce change and health in that child's life. Paul's admonition to the church in Corinth that they put the man involved in an incestuous relationship out of the church, is an example of "tough love" (1 Corinthians 5:5).

Having said all this, the real question isn't whether or not we love our church, or its older and slower-to-adapt members. Of course we must love them, which means we do what's best for them. What's best is always to obey Christ and his call to keep the two greatest commandments and the great commission. The real question is how we show compassion and comfort to them while leading them down this sometimes difficult path.

I'm reminded of a parenting example. If my kids did something wrong, I would tell them and redirect them in the right way. If they listened and tried to do it, I would praise and assist them. If they told me to drop dead, I had a different reaction. But even in those times of punitive action, upon seeing tears, or a repentant spirit, I would always hug and comfort. Why is leadership of the family of God any different?

We must always teach and lead with patience. We empathize with the difficulty and pain of the change. If people try and fail, we pick them up and hug them while giving them pointers along the way. If they rebel, we correct them with church discipline and pray for repentance. If repentance occurs, we forgive and forget. If repentance does not occur, they must move on and we trust that God will perfect them elsewhere. This is love, and therefore loving.

Church discipline is a forgotten and rarely practiced art in today's church. Still, loving discipline is the basis for a church transformation and, frankly, it's the basis for the rest of this book.

I could no doubt write a separate book on each of these doctrinal issues. Still, for the sake of brevity, I've listed them basically, as illustrations and "food for thought." I think evidence exists showing that without these and perhaps other doctrinal clarifications and adjustments, pain and failure are virtually guaranteed.

Chapter 5

Crucify Your Church Structurally

E ven though we touched on this in an earlier chapter, the subject of structure warrants special attention. This is, in my opinion, one of the most critical areas of change necessary to the rebirth of a church.

Historically, the largest Protestant denominations in America patterned their organizations, not along biblical lines, but by following a liberal interpretation of the democratic system in the Constitution of the United States. Perhaps this is due to the fact that within the original thirteen colonies, the state and federal documents ultimately used to formulate our country's constitution and the Bill of Rights were often drafted (you guessed it) in churches. It follows that, as these churches were established and spread from east to west, this democratic form of polity would also spread.

Now while it's true that the U.S. constitution's structure is actually a representative republic, not a true democracy (thus more presbyterian than congregational), the push for freedom has caused a shift both in our political interpretation of it (as seen in the current presidential administration) and in our religious use of polity for the church. Regardless of how it started, the parallels between our American government and our predominantly baptistic and congregational church culture are unquestionable.

And while the timing of church versus U.S. political structure may be a "chicken and egg" question, the bottom line is that the decision to adopt a modified version of U.S. political structure, over time, has brought both good news and bad news into the church. The good news is that these Congregational and Baptist churches were often less prone to abuse by powerful clergymen since these clergymen were, in essence, stripped of any real authority. They also experienced a higher degree of involvement than did some Catholic or Anglican churches, for instance, because all members had "a say" and a share or stake in the church's day-to-day business.

Congregationalists argue to this day that their structure increases involvement and helps create a sense of ownership. The question is, at what cost? Most pastors would much rather see people serving in ministries they are gifted for rather than wasting hours in unproductive committee meetings. And regarding ownership, who really owns the church? Isn't it Jesus? So if we make people think the church belongs to them and thus, that it exists to do their bidding, isn't that a problem?

I would argue, and I believe history unquestionably affirms, that the bad news concerning congregational or democratic polity *far* outweighs the good. After all, the church of Jesus Christ is a theocracy, not a humanly devised democracy. This is a distinction we cannot take lightly, no matter how abusive a priest or episcopally ordered leader may be.

I recently reread the story of Korah's rebellion in Numbers 16. I was shocked to see the similarity between Korah's justification of that action and the standard congregational use of 1 Peter 2:9. Korah said to Moses, "You have gone too far. The whole community is holy. Why then do you set yourselves above the Lord's assembly?" Isn't this the same argument Congregationalist churches make regarding the "priesthood of all believers?" Is it not the same logic that makes the pastor's vote the same value as anyone else's?

In congregationally governed churches, pastors thus become chaplains. They can pray, visit, preach, teach, and do baby dedications, yet they must *never* exercise authority for discipline, strategy, leadership, management of staff or volunteers, and so on. But how does this jibe with Hebrews 13:17, where all church members are told to obey their leaders? This is hard when they think they themselves *are* the leaders!

Problems associated with congregational governance include:

- **The "inmates running the asylum."** People with one week's experience as a Christian often have the same vote on major issues as does their pastor. His years of experience, theology degree(s), and his spiritual maturity are irrelevant in the process.

   Once we had a constitutionally mandated vote regarding the hiring of a part-time choir director (in itself an absurd requirement). The chairman of the worship committee and I both interviewed the candidate and felt she was a perfect fit. Both of us would work with her and she would ultimately report to me. Incidentally, I also have a music background and thus felt comfortable making the decision. I just wasn't allowed to. Instead, more than fifty people each had an equal vote on whether or not we would hire a person they had never met or interviewed. During the meeting, one member stood and comically objected, "I don't even know the man," only to be elbowed by his wife who reminded him that our candidate was a woman. So my opinion of the candidate was of equal value to that of an individual who didn't even know the candidate's gender. Don't get me wrong, I love this man—he's a great guy and a solid believer. He just didn't have time to get the information about the candidate. The point is that many ill-equipped, ill-informed, and sometimes spiritually immature people have as much authority as would a biblical elder, in a congregationally governed church. Ultimately, this cannot work to accomplish the goals given to us by our Lord.

- **Division.** Whenever you vote, someone loses (unless it's unanimous). Voting automatically divides people. The sad history of congregational denominations is that thousands of churches have been born out of divisive splits over the color of the pews, the time of service, who should serve on this or that board, or other mundane issues. What message does this send to a lost and dying world?

  Manipulation. In one local congregation, there was a vote recently on leaving their denomination over theological differences. Their constitution, however, maintained that once one became a member, it was a lifetime position. A campaign thus ensued to invite people to vote who hadn't set foot in the church for years. One lady, who hadn't been to the church building for any reason for over twenty-five years, came and voted to stay with the denomination. While the pastoral staff and deacons had biblical reasons for leaving, their recommendation was initially voted down! The church remained affiliated until a later date when a new vote could be taken and thus was cast to overturn the first one.

Spiritual abuse. Ironically, the system designed to prevent abuse is responsible for creating more abuse than other political structures. For example, one of our churches had a so-called "nominating committee." One week, we had prospective members share their testimonies before being voted into membership by those attending a special meeting after church. The problem was that the deacons and I hadn't noticed that the fine print of our constitution mandated that these events occur "during a regularly scheduled business meeting or worship service." Our services had technically ended before the sharing time, so our nominating committee chairman refused to recognize the membership status of the new converts and thus ruled them ineligible to serve. Legalism and power-grabbing are commonplace in this form of polity. The sad truth is that it's often the newer Christians or visitors who get hurt in the process.

- **Wasted resources.** Often it takes months or even years to do what the rest of the world could accomplish in days. Church leaders aren't allowed to lead and volunteers waste countless hours in meetings, only to see things "tabled for prayer" again and again and again.

Once, our church decided, finally, to rewrite our constitution, the board assigned the task of creating a draft constitution to the constitution committee. At first, this almost made sense until they too formed an "ad hoc subcommittee" that decided that, since there is safety in numbers, they would write the new document as a group project. Ultimately the chairman of that ad hoc subcommittee left the church and we didn't see even a draft for over two years! I'm ashamed of how we wasted our Lord's resources in this process.

On another occasion, our denomination decided to "fix" a problem caused by perceived poor management by a director over one of its ministries. The solution was the creation of a new oversight board and at least three new committees to direct the new director. We now had more than twenty people doing one person's job—what a waste! How much better would it be to just replace the ineffective leader with someone better suited to the task?

I'd be remiss if I didn't address the problems with many mainline polities as well. A purely episcopal or denominationally presbyterian polity is never flawless either. Often this is because what's in the statement of faith or articles of incorporation is rarely what is practiced in real life. What I mean is that just because the doctrinal statement says we follow a "biblical structure," it doesn't mean we actually do this in our day-to-day operations. An episcopal form may lend itself to embracing tyrants at times. This is bad.

On the other hand, we all know that sometimes a local parish may take more control such that the priest or pastor becomes little more than a figurehead. The Presbyterian form may be closer to the biblical "mark," but many Presbyterian churches are led by people who have been given more authority than their constitution suggests. For that matter, many Baptist or Congregational churches give over complete authority to a charismatic leader who can then dominate in an unhealthy way, *despite* what their legal charter says.

What's the answer?

I could go on and on, but more importantly, what is the biblical view and teaching on this subject? What is most obedient to Scripture and thus, will produce fruit, once a church is reborn? Many books have been written on polity and it's not my intent to explore all the subtleties of each form. I will say that Scripture is clear that churches were led by elders and those elders were assisted by deacons. (See appendix ii and iii for definitions of each role. We've used these as handouts to help church members understand them more clearly in the past.)

In our modern context, some or even all of those elders may be paid staff. If so, it would make sense to empower them to make the day-to-day decisions necessary to accomplish kingdom work, with the lead or senior pastor having more authority than other staff members. Rick Warren describes much of this in great detail in his book, *The Purpose Driven Church*. It is also important to eliminate some of the other problems we've discussed, while avoiding abuses by elders in the process.

At Mill Pond Church, we've tried to avoid extremes by empowering elders, while recognizing the senior pastor's lead role. (See appendix i, *Mill Pond Church Constitution*.) Regarding congregational input/authority, to avoid division, we only vote on three things:

1. The purchase of real estate.
2. A change to our constitution.

3. Replacing the senior pastor (but not on replacing other staff).

This helps us avoid division caused by the voting process. But how do we encourage participation? Simple. We empower people to run their ministries as our elders administer doctrine and run the day-to-day operations of the church. We get things done, all are involved, and we avoid spiritual abuse in large part. Still, we preach that "every member is a minister" and we involve people, as Rick Warren puts it, in ministry not maintenance. Thus, instead of being tied up in meetings, people are busy doing what God has gifted them to do.

Before I close this chapter, I must do a reality check. In the vast majority of cases, the chances of you prying the golden scepter of power out of member's or non-elder lay leader's hands are like my chances of replacing the Dalai Lama as a non-Buddhist. Furthermore, if you're under an episcopal or presbyterian form and you know changes need to be made to become staff-led (or to make some other power shift), that's going to be tough. There may even be legal or denominational constraints on what you're allowed to do "on paper."

If you're in this kind of situation, one option may be to embrace the reality of the spirit of the law versus the letter. For example, in Connecticut, the speed limit is 55 on some highways. Still, traveling at just 55 is a form of vehicular suicide. You see, everyone knows that the *real*, unwritten speed limit is actually 60–65 and no self-respecting state trooper will pull you over for driving at that speed in a 55 zone. So, most travel at 65, while a car moving at 55 will be virtually run off the road.

My point?

If the written constitution of your church isn't really being followed today (as with an episcopal form of polity, with no empowered priest) your *new* form of polity may be different, even if your constitution can't change. So while your denominational paperwork says one thing, if your local body supports a more biblical approach, you can live that way without trouble. I know that what I'm suggesting is risky, but at the end of the day, who would you rather anger—your bishop or Jesus?

When our Lord returns will He say, "Well done, good and faithful servant—you kept to your constitution and lived it 'to a T?'" I doubt it. His affirmation will come for those who obey the Great Commandments and the Great Commission, not the Great Constitution!

Along these lines, don't fall prey to what I call "the FUD Factory." Prior to being a fulltime pastor, I worked in sales and marketing, primarily in the computer industry. Once, we ran an ad in several computer publications showing a factory on a hill spewing smoke clouds with the word FUD inside. As the ad explained, "FUD stands for fear, uncertainty, and doubt." Our competition would use these three elements to cast doubt on our products and we were, in essence, fighting back by telling people not to listen to FUD.

The problem is that many churches run on FUD. When we were trying to function within the legalistic constraints of our constitution at Community Church (CC), people would often tell me that the state of Connecticut would "shut us down" or "arrest our leaders" if we didn't follow the bylaws in excruciating detail. I did some checking on this and found that not only did the state not have a copy of our constitution and bylaws; they had no interest in them. In other words, what we did or didn't do in terms of how or when we welcomed members into fellowship, voted on the purchase of Silly Putty, and the like, was of no consequence to Connecticut. Thus, no SWAT teams were going to drive up in vans, or rappel down from black helicopters onto our lawn, because we let the pastor hire a worship leader without a congregational vote.

Because I can already hear it ringing in my ears, let me be clear that I'm not suggesting lawlessness, nor am I saying we should take legal risks. What I am saying is that there are times, especially when the details are unclear, that we can live in the spirit or intent of the "law" without having to go through the pain of a constitutional rewrite or a denominational split. If this applies, do it and don't let FUD stop you.

At one point in our transition at CC, I remember standing in front of the congregation with a Bible in one hand and a copy of our constitution in the other. I boldly and loudly asked them, "Which are we going to follow, church?" Then, I took the constitution and threw it into the pews and said, "As long as I'm your pastor, we'll follow Scripture first. If that's not acceptable, fire me now!" Surprisingly, I got a standing ovation. I'd like to tell you that I always stood this strong on such matters, but that would be a lie. At that point, I'd had enough. The good news is that most of our members had too!

I remember talking to a deacon in one of the oldest churches in our city. At 65 years old, he was the youngest member of their struggling church of about twelve people. "

We blew it," he told me. "We stopped doing the soup kitchens and serving the community several years ago. We had the perfect spot and yet we turned inward and we blew it." Again, this is why churches must die first— sometimes literally folding up to allow a new, younger leadership team to use the property, or the proceeds from its sale, to start fresh. Sometimes, it's just not possible to change what needs to change. To his credit, he and the other members were passionate about making sure their property would be owned by a younger, more outwardly focused church. They wanted to be sure that whoever took over their building would not make the same mistakes they had.

There are several paradigm shifts you must make to restructure effectively:

•**Team versus Committee.** In a classic committee, everyone is equal and equivalent. Decisions are made as a group, so everyone has an equal "say" and an equal vote. On a team, there's a captain and everyone on the team functions based on giftedness. In basketball, for example, not everyone is the center. Each has his "position" to play.

•**Leader versus Chairman.** A chairman is a facilitator. He has little power other than force of personality. A leader, like a quarterback, makes calls and runs the offense. He has authority. He uses it to get the most out of the abilities of each teammate.

•**Mission versus Meeting.** In this paradigm, the team knows that they exist to accomplish Matthew 28:19–20. They don't see the meeting as an end—rather; it is a means to an end. In contrast, the purpose of committees is to meet once a month and discuss issues (often only to then table them for a later time). A ministry team, on the other hand, sees accomplishing a goal as primary. If they can do it without meetings, they will. It's a matter of per-spective and priority.

•**Message versus Method.** The gospel must be preserved while our means of sharing it must change. The infirmity of the modern church comes from changing the gospel mes-sage, while ignorantly maintaining old, outdated methods.

•**Truth versus Tradition.** At Mill Pond Church, we say "there are no sacred cows, but if we ever find one, we'll have a barbeque!" Traditions are fine, but *truth* is the focus. If a tradition supports and promotes truth, it can stay. Otherwise, it must be sacrificed.

•**Relationships versus Religion.** The overriding, and perhaps most important, paradigm shift necessary is to see the Great Commandment of Matthew 28 as primary—even over the Great Commission, because the Great Commission results from the love of God and others (especially "lost" others). If people never "get" the idea of connecting personally with God and experiencing ever-deepening relationships with others—the church is an utter failure. Religion kills—relationships give life!

So try to change paradigms and then try to change structure. Rewrite your constitution or charter if necessary. But if all else fails, just know that even if the church "closes," new birth is possible—and in Christ—it's inevitable!

Chapter 6

Crucify Your Church with Vision

Proverbs 29:18 says, "Where *there is* no vision, the people perish: but he that keepeth the law, happy *is* he (KJV)." Lamentations 2:9 tells of a time when the people of God were devastated. Jeremiah writes, "...her kings and her princes are among the Gentiles...her prophets find no vision from the Lord (KJV)."

Rarely are these verses quoted in context and that in itself is quite revealing. You see, the connection between the written law (Word of God), and vision is absolute and inextricable! It's in vogue today, however, to develop our own personalized vision—one seemingly "unique," "hip and happening," "post-modern." or "cool." But why? Aren't the Great Commandments and the Great Commission good enough? Do we *really* think we can "one-up" God?

Once we've developed that sexy new vision statement, does it run the risk of trumping what God has already provided as marching orders for his Bride? Yes! And whether it's written or memorized, posted on church letterhead and business cards, or just "understood" like some unspoken rule—a vision that's not clearly from Scripture can, and likely will, destroy a church.

That's one of several reasons why vision must sometimes die before a new, healthy vision can even be cast, let alone pursued.

In my experience, we have several problematic tendencies here.

1. **To ignore former, "hidden agenda" visions, or even written ones when planting a new vision.** We assume the new one will trump the old, but often the old lives on, causing confusion. It's as if our town posted two different speed limit signs on the same street. At CC, I made this mistake by ignoring the *real* underlying vision of the church and its leaders. The real vision was to preserve CC and its 118-year heritage at all costs. For instance, since the church had several teachers in the leadership, its vision was to teach, not necessarily to reach new people, since new people only make a mess. To our established members, the five purposes

of Matthew 22 and Matthew 28 (worship, ministry, evangelism, discipleship, and fellowship) were just a means to an end, not *the* end!

2. **To knowingly take on a new vision, while intentionally keeping the old.** Even if they are synergistic, the resulting confusion is the same as in number 1 above.

3. **To kill the first vision and cast a new one without explaining why the first needed to go.** If it's arbitrary and seemingly random, people expect that the same thing could happen at any moment to the new vision. There needs to be a clear and complete dissatisfaction with the old vision, thus prompting its execution, in favor of a new, clearly scriptural one (death and resurrection).

4. **To forget or fail to explain that not only will the old vision die, but the new vision will likely necessitate the death of many ministries, traditions, constitutions, and more, before the rebirth is over.** If it's good, vision will crucify your church and give birth to a new, healthier, growing body. People have a right to know and prayerfully commit to that tsunami before it hits.

I think that number 4 was my biggest leadership mistake in each of the church transitions I led. I tried to ease the church into change or even pretend that it wouldn't be that big a deal. I assumed the new vision would be followed and people would gleefully embrace the Great Commission, such that any changes we'd experience would be "hardly noticeable." Right! Actually, this naiveté nearly destroyed my ministry. In hindsight, I now believe it would be better to call an all-church meeting, give them all a cup of coffee, sit them down, and say,

"Attention members—we've decided to crucify our church, its vision, its ministries, and anything else that gets in the way. Then, once the carnage is over and it's all dead and buried, we'll start a new church based exclusively on Matthew 22 and 28."

Is this shocking? Sure! But is it truthful? Absolutely. And any fallout from this meeting will likely be less than, or the same as, what would eventually result from a slow, agonizing, painful process of change. Yet, that slow transition is what most pundits and self-proclaimed gurus recommend.

Clearly, I wouldn't recommend literally saying, "Attention members—we've decided to crucify our church..." It's more than a bit too strong. Still, the idea is that it's better for leaders to honestly deal with the challenge of change than to sugar-coat it and attempt to minimize its impact. It's better to talk about the death of church and it's rebirth than to pretend that it won't be painful and all-encompassing.

I would add here that the same is true of mergers. My second biggest mistake at CC was thinking that we could merge three churches together into some kind of hybrid triad. I thought we could take the strengths of each and then sort of negate or delete the weaknesses. The truth is, New Born church was young and founded on principles that made her the healthiest and strongest of the three. Yet even she had to die to make this work—even though she was the dominant force in the merger. Regardless, the other two churches had to die to self and submit to New Born and her leaders to make the merger work. Since the merger, I've heard several other Christian leaders say the same thing—mergers are typically takeovers and constitute a new beginning for all concerned. Thus, the faster they happen, the better!

I think it's like gall bladder surgery. Which would you prefer?

A. Your doctor opens a partial hole in your body and takes the rest of the day off. In a day or two, he comes back to see if you've survived, and gives you some morphine. Then, he finishes the full incision before taking a thirty-minute coffee break. After the break, he chats with you a while and plays a game of Scrabble with you and the nursing staff. He then takes a vacation, and after a week, comes back and removes your gall bladder. Following the removal, he leaves the hole open and plays golf with some friends for two days. When he returns, he finds you wrenching in agony. So, rather than stress you further, he puts a bandage on you and postpones the rest of the surgery so they can treat the infections caused by the open wound, and so on. Or,

B. The surgeon knocks you out, cuts you open, removes the infected gall bladder, closes you up, and has you in recovery within a couple of hours?

Obviously, we would all prefer B. Yet many church renewals take seven years or more. In fact, many "experts" recommend taking even more time. Are you kidding me? What's even more shocking is that the successful churches still lose an average of 50 percent of their original members! How foolish—why not cut her open, do the job, sew her up, and move on already? It's better for the church and it's definitely better for the thousands of unchurched, lost people who won't get saved while we're prolonging the agony of a gentle transition or a vision change.

And by the way, the age-old analogy of the frog in the boiling water is antithetical to those who support gradual change. You know the story—if you drop a frog in hot water, he'll jump out, but if you slowly turn up the temperature, one degree at a time over several hours, he'll boil alive and not even notice. The problem with using this analogy to support a slow transition is that at the end of it, the frog isn't reborn or transformed—he's cooked! Furthermore, I'd rather have people hop out, than to stay and be miserable. So, again, go as fast as you can and get it over with.

Now this doesn't mean that you ignore or avoid teaching and mentoring along the way. I admit, that *does* take time. But it's time to teach the reasons for change and then facilitate change as quickly as possible. It's not time to slowly "boil" your church by tricking them into a transition they will ultimately rebel against. In my experience, the slow change process doesn't work anyway, so why not teach them, restructure, pray, and move on? (See chapter 9.)

Who's the Vision For?

I once asked a pastor friend about his vision for his community. "I don't have one," he said honestly. "My job is to care for the flock." While I appreciated his honesty, (especially in contrast to most who wouldn't admit this, even though that's exactly how they feel), it's a sad contrast to the biblical mandate to impact the whole world, not just our "holy huddle."

If your vision is good and if it's scriptural, it will apply to you, your members, your kids, your visitors, your city, your state, your region—your world! As such it needs to be shared with everyone, every chance you get!

While it's not my purpose to tell you how to write your vision (partially because I think God has already done that for us), I will say that you need to keep it short, yet clear, and easily repeatable so that you can repeat it often and have it easily understood. For example, Mill Pond Church's vision is simply, "To passionately love God, then actively love people."

Does that need explanation? Not really. It warrants fleshing out, showing *how* the five biblical purposes flow from it, but it's pretty darn clear all by itself. In fact, it's just a paraphrase of the Great Commandments and the Great Commission.

Vision Flow

Finally, on this topic, I'd like to address the flow of vision development, vision casting, vision ownership, and vision implementation. I'm convinced that good vision never flows from a brainstorming session with the entire church sitting in a room with a flip chart. I know—I'm a radical—but that's just an angry mob rebelling against God's vision. Sorry…but I'm convinced that they wouldn't even be having their brainstorming session if they accepted what God had already given as sufficient. Do we really believe that 100 people arguing linguistics can do better than, "Go…make disciples…?"

Of course not!

I believe our vision exists in scripture. Further, I believe it is the senior pastor's job—just as in a sermon—to interpret that scripture and contextualize it, presenting it in a culturally relevant way to the flock. Of course, as we've already discussed, he should have killed the old vision first.

At this point in the process, the flock has a choice. They can rebel against what God has said (since the vision is from Scripture, let's not mince words), or they can follow it. Those who choose to follow can help form vision leadership and implementation teams. And, off we go!

Even pastors who play what I call, "the vision discovery game" (pretending to start with a blank page and developing a "unique" vision for "our church")—if they are men of integrity—will ultimately come back to Scripture anyway. In essence, they just end up rewording God's command so as to appease the need to be "different from all those other churches."

So why not start there? Why not openly use Scripture? If your flock is composed of sheep, they'll follow. If it's not composed of sheep, they won't anyway, so why waste time? Tell the truth—the vision is from God's Word and it's His—period! Our job is simply to carry it out. Any other vision must be removed and put to death.

Again, this was one of my major errors both at the Worldwide Church of God (WCG) and at CC. I tried playing the vision discovery game and, in retrospect, it just made matters worse.

Before closing this chapter, let me be clear that I do believe a vision can be applied and contextualized in a unique way, based on the community and a church's gifting. Still, this is a pragmatic and tactical uniqueness, not a truly unique mission and vision. For example, at Mill Pond Church, we have worded ours as a short and sweet summary of the Great Commission and Great Commandment. It's along the lines of what is recommended in the book *Simple Church*. 11 Why? Because we're dealing with a sound bite driven culture of young people who wouldn't read a fifty-word mission or vision statement anyway.

"Passionately loving God, then actively loving people," says the same thing as Matthew 22 and Matthew 28, in a condensed way. We didn't reinvent God's vision—we just presented it in a culturally relevant way. It didn't take fifty people with a flip chart several weeks to do this. It just sort of happened as we studied Scripture and tried to explain it to our troops.

Chapter 7

Crucify Your Church through Missions

It's probably easier to talk about what missions isn't, than to start with what missions is. Missions, in biblical terms, aren't sending money to parachurch organizations to do what we refuse to do as churches. Missions isn't sending Sunday School teachers to a third-world country to do what indigenous Christian leaders can and should be doing anyway. Missions isn't what 75 percent of most church "missions" budgets are spent on!

Do I have your attention yet?

Missions is church planting and multiplication—period! "What?" you may ask. "Isn't that a bit narrow?"

A careful study of the book of Acts shows that the apostles never won souls without also gathering them, establishing them with sound doctrine, naming and ordaining elders, and continuing to follow up to ensure health and growth. In other words, they planted churches! And, that's all they did because they apparently believed that having healthy churches throughout the Roman Empire would be enough to transform that empire—and history proves they were right!

Apparently, Peter, John, James, Paul, and others had the idea that the local church was the hope of a sick, pluralistic, godless, Roman culture. They actually believed that if they established churches in places like Rome, Corinth, Ephesus, and Antioch, those cities would be better off and their personal Great Commission call would be completed.

Apparently the apostles didn't get the memo about starting foreign missions agencies, denominations, college campus ministries, men's and women's ministries, children's ministries, medical outreach groups, and a host of other parachurch organizations to do what the church could and should have been doing in the first place!

And we're here because of it!

Far from silly, the approach of first-century church leaders was inspired. Our problem is that we've forgotten it. Billy Graham is reported to have said that if the church did her job; his entire evangelistic association would be unnecessary and thus nonexistent. To this I shout, "Amen!"

I believe that the church has abdicated her role and then established missions funds to assuage her guilt by sending money to others who will do it for her. It's like a dad who pays his secretary to buy toys for his neglected kid's birthday. He feels good by attempting to buy his son's affection and he doesn't have to do the work!

Dream with me for a moment…

What if a local church "owned" its community? If it was located near a college, they would try to connect with students intentionally, lead them to Christ, and have them join the church. Then, what if, instead of sending money to InterVarsity, Campus Crusade, Navigators, or whomever, they used the students they mentored to reach other students and maybe even started a weekly remote worship site on campus? Can you see it? (I've got goose bumps here.) What if they eventually hired a leader (maybe even one of the campus ministry guys from a parachurch group), to be on staff so he didn't have to spend 50 percent of his time fundraising or working? What if that happened in every church in every city in every country where a college campus existed?

Bless God—we're having a revival meeting here!

Not only would those churches grow, but the students would connect to older and younger folks in authentic community. Shucks—they might even join those churches and stay there instead of disappearing until they hit thirty and have kids of their own.

If you're not excited yet, you should be! This illustration only scratches the surface of what could happen if churches took ownership of the Great Commission in their communities. We've only looked at college outreach. Now add every ethnic group, age, gender—outreach to every imaginable demographic description and you've got the picture.

Globally, what if, instead of sending short-term or long-term missionaries to third-world countries to carry buckets of sand to build schools, we sent church planters (or better yet—worked with indigenous church planters) to start and establish churches who would do *much* more than what we could ever do ourselves? What if those new, indigenous churches then "owned" their communities?

Now can you feel it?

What if the average fee of $2,000 per person spent on a week-long "mission" to some foreign land went to the indigenous pastor who would then multiply campuses—and churches hundredfold? What if the 20 to 30 percent of budget most churches spent on "missions" actually resulted in new converts, new campuses, or new churches? We *know* that church planting is the most effective means of evangelism. Therefore, could the Great Commission be fulfilled sooner? Could our Lord's return thus be imminent?

Like our churches, our view of missions must die so that something better can be born. Like a butterfly, that new mission will be much prettier and effective than the ugly, slow-moving caterpillar of the old view of missions.

Paul and his teams planted more than thirty churches, which quickly multiplied into hundreds. This is a conservative number, because the original thirty were "city churches" composed of what most scholars agree were many house-churches in each city. By the third century, hundreds of city churches saturated the Roman Empire.

Paul's method of entering a community, finding God-fearers, making disciples, gathering disciples into congregations, raising up and ordaining elders, and then starting again elsewhere while still visiting and writing to the churches already established, *has never been improved upon*. This is what the missionaries must do on foreign or native soil!

This is missions!

Now, just to clarify and avoid hate mail, am I saying we should immediately and suddenly close all parachurch organizations or stop supporting pseudo-missionaries? No. What I *am* saying is that church planting and establishment should once again become our priority. From that, a gradual assimilation of these organizations and missionaries into local churches would inevitably occur as their tasks began to be completed by those same churches.

Also to clarify, I am *not* saying that this focus negates feeding the hungry, helping with disaster relief in foreign countries, supporting the medical work of groups like Mercy Ships, and so on. What I am saying is that nobody is biblically and practically better equipped to do these things than an indigenous local church. So the epicenter of missions is church planting. It always has been and, I hope again soon, will always be!

Chapter 8

Crucify Your Church Via a New Name

One of the most charming promises in the New Testament is that of receiving a new name. It makes sense. What is a new identity, a fresh start, a new beginning, if we carry with us the old name and all that is attached to it?

In Scripture, names are more than significant—they are critical. God always names things commensurate with their current identity. Think of God giving Saul the name Paul, once he was born anew. Names in the Bible connote character, personality, calling, and are also prophetic as to an individual's future. There's more I could say here, but let's cut to the chase. If people get a new name because they've been born anew and their old name is now irrelevant, then why not churches?

Whether or not a church's original name had purposeful significance and regardless of the church's track record in fulfilling that significance—the changes we've outlined so far in this book *demand* a new identity and name. If a church has died and been born again, it must have a new name.

Why?

Old names carry with them old expectations, denominational and traditional baggage, and more. When we faced the merger of Community Church (CC) and the other two churches, we wrestled with this. One thing we knew was that in our context, we had to remove the name of our denomination in order to reach some of the people we were called to reach. Still, to our older members, this idea was like amputating a limb! What I explained to them was that most new, unchurched people who saw the name of our denomination on our sign would ask me questions such as:

- "Does joining your church mean I can't have wine at my daughter's wedding?"
- "Does this mean I'll never dance or go to movies again?"
- "Another church from your denomination told me I had to read the King James Bible, but I couldn't understand it. Is that a requirement at your church too?"

Since none of these things applied in our church, the connotations were untrue. Thus, the name needed to change.

In the end, we adopted the name of one of the other churches involved in the merger, since that church was only seven years old. It's name was new, fresh, and their reputation was powerful in our city. New Born was a name that reflected what was happening in the merger, and what we prayed for in the lives of all we met.

New Born Church, while new, had loved and reached out so often that they were more widely known than our 118-year old church. They were known as a caring, serving, evangelizing group of Christians. Even if all this weren't in the picture, however, I liked their name and believed it fit the situation. With all that was changing, New Born seemed to fit.

But it's not just the name of the church that needs to change. The far-reaching effects of a death and rebirth normally require a whole new vocabulary regarding buildings, ministries, and even staff titles, etc. In our case, the "narthex" became the "lobby," the "sanctuary" became an "auditorium, "Sunday School" became "Kidz Church." and "Fellowship Hall" became "the Café."

The point is that names matter, so be willing to change. And in that vein, be sure that the new names you choose reflect what God is doing, not just what is "hip" or "cool." If the goal is the Great Commission, names will make sense to unchurched people too—not just to the folks who speak what I call "Christianese."

In summary, the new names and vocabulary criteria include:

- Making sure the name is scripturally reflective of your new identity.
- Making sure the new name is easy for unchurched people to comprehend without misunderstanding, whenever possible.
- Making sure the new name is as timeless as possible.

Chapter 9

What Do I Do First?

've tried hard to stay principle-centered in this book so far. Most of us are sick of being given glitzy marketing packages with simplistic formulas on "How to Grow a Big Church" or "How to Transform Your Church into a Virtual Saddleback in Three Easy Steps!" Still, the question of where to start is legitimate. If you've decided to crucify your church, what do you do first?

I would suggest that you view it like building a house. Jesus taught that the foundation was the most important thing. While the specifics will vary from congregation to congregation, I think you must start with doctrine. What things are you doing or teaching that contradict scripture?

When the Worldwide Church of God underwent its massive doctrinal overhaul, Pastor General Joseph Tkach, Sr., told those of us in the ministry that nothing was going to be held to, unless it was found in and clearly supported by Scripture. In other words, there were no doctrinal "sacred cows." If it was in the Bible, we'd teach it and live it. If it wasn't in Scripture, contradicted Scripture, or made it hard to obey Scripture, we'd get rid of it. And *boy*—he meant it!

Over the next few years, virtually every major doctrine of our church came under scrutiny. Now, we were a cult, so *everything* changed. Clearly, I'm not suggesting that will happen to your church. Still, as we illustrated in chapter 4, there are bound to be areas of theology where you need to fine tune, if not completely rebuild and repair.

These doctrinal changes are the easiest to make. Why? Because you'll have clear scriptural support as the basis for them. People may not like change, but if they're saved, they'll dislike arguing with God even more. If you clearly show them in Scripture where change is needed, they may not like it, but they'll ultimately go along. The real hard changes are the more subtle, subjective ones like chairs versus pews. The good news is that starting with doctrine makes everything else flow a bit easier.

For most churches, I would suppose that the primary doctrinal change will center-around the Great Commission. For many, the Great Commission has become the "Great Omission." So before you launch a new outreach campaign or teach the "Contagious Christian" class by Bill Hybels, you may need to biblically teach through what Jesus and the apostles said about winning the lost.

Now, let's return to our home building analogy. Once you've laid a solid foundation, you work on the framework or structure. For most churches this is polity. You may need to rewrite your constitution. If this isn't possible, you can have a "gentleman's agreement" with your leaders about how you'll implement or apply the truths of Scripture, despite your constitution or charter. The bottom line is that until you agree on *how* you'll do business, you'll be unable to move forward to change the other things which need to change.

The main issue with structural change is that leaders need to be empowered to lead. Otherwise, change is impossible. The idea that you can politic and campaign a crowd into voting changes into place may have some merit, but it takes forever and is exhausting, if it works at all. In order to complete a healthy rebirth, a church must empower elders and other leaders who can teach the Scripture and then make decisions in obedience to that Scripture. Will they teach the congregation first? Yes, thus the foundation, above. But, when push (maybe literally) comes to shove, the leaders must have the authority to make decisions and move forward.

Mob rule often moves in the wrong direction. Furthermore, even when the "mob" eventually moves in the right direction, the time and energy it takes will lead to burnout. Thousands of pastors have quit or taken early retirement as a result of this kind of exhausting effort.

Let me add a word about spiritual abuse or bullying. Some have suggested that if a pastor or elder board makes decisions against the will of the congregation, they're bullying. I disagree. Bullying has to do with motive, attitude, and approach to implementation, *not* the decision itself.

For example, if a family votes over dinner choices each day, it's likely that the 4, 6, and 8-year old kids will outnumber mom and dad. It's also likely that a vote for m&m's instead of chicken wouldn't be the best choice for their health. So, what do loving, empowered parents do? They teach and gently overrule. That's not bullying—it's leadership.

Now if mom and dad scream, slam the table, and force-feed green beans to the kids by stuffing them down their little throats—that's bullying! But gently explaining, serving chicken, and modeling how to eat a balanced diet, is not. That's just good leadership. Now if the kids ultimately refuse to eat and "cop an attitude" in rebellion and nastiness at the table, there may need to be other consequences. Still, those are also carried out with firm, loving leadership.

Church leaders need to be empowered and then have the guts to do the same with the sheep in their flock. So when the church wants to keep the name, "First Intergenerational Denominational Congregational Church of the Holy

Ecclesiology" and the pastor and elders know that this has about as much value in reaching lost souls as would conducting animal sacrifices in the parking lot—they need to gently explain the logic, make the name change, and comfort those who grieve, while moving forward. And, if a few sheep get nasty (proving they're goats after all), the shepherds need to remove them from the flock after trying gently and graciously to help them change.

What about the home-building roof? I believe the roof is worship. If you don't have a prayer team—form one. If your worship leaders don't understand what it means to be in the Lord's presence, find one who does or buy every song by Hillsongs and similar groups. You *need* Spirit-led worship. You need a prayer covering. Jim Cymbala's book, *Fresh Wind, Fresh Fire* is a great book to help you make prayer the priority in your church.13 Whatever you need to do, beyond doctrine and polity, it will flow much easier if you have biblical worship in place.

The other benefit of this worship "roof" is that it will allow you to hear from God so that you can best determine the priorities for the remainder of your transition. If you need to deal with a new name or form some new ministries or "Crucify" your missions strategy, the Spirit of God will lead into the proper order and then help you with all the details. They say that "the devil's in the details," and I agree. That is just one more reason why we must bring the power of the Holy Spirit with us under our roof of worship. Once you have that—everything else is just drywall and decoration.

Chapter 10

OBJECTIONS!

I love movies, especially dramas. Courtroom dramas intrigue me because I've often thought that if I wasn't a pastor, I could have been a lawyer. In those movies and TV shows depicting courtroom battles, whenever an attorney says or asks something inappropriate question, the opposing lawyer will scream, "OBJECTION!"

Some of you are yelling, "OBJECTION!" even now.

I realize that the ideas proposed in this book are radical. Some of them fly in the face of things we were taught in cemetery, er I mean, seminary. I'm pretty straightforward, so let me throw out some of the most common objections you might get, and how to reply to them. Here are the top ten objections to "The Crucified Church."

1. Pastor Joel, you're just angry about past church stuff. Why not just leave it alone?

If you haven't read the foreword to this book, please take a minute to do so now. I'd be lying if I didn't say that I was or have been angry about some of what has happened in my ministry career. Still, I can just as quickly and forthrightly say that I'm honestly and decidedly not angry now.

The motivation for this book is to foster change in the Body of Christ. I love the church! I just love what God called her to be more than what she is now. That's why I can't just leave it alone. I've tried that (*we've* tried that!) and it's not working.

2. Jesus said the "gates of hell shall not prevail" against the church. How can you say it's dying?

I'll let the cold, hard facts of research done by far greater men than I speak for themselves regarding the true state of the twenty-first century church in America and Western Europe. Still, I should make it clear that I firmly believe that when Jesus said that even the gates of hell wouldn't prevail against the Church, He meant it (Matthew 16:18, KJV)!

The church in Asia, Africa, India, and South America is growing by leaps and bounds. Some estimate that more than 10,000 people a day are being saved in Asia.12 So the worldwide church isn't dying—nor will she. In these places, she's been reborn and I pray she will be reborn here as well.

3. What if they fire me?

One of my current ministry "hats" is that I act as "director of multiplication" for Converge Northeast. I'm basically the church-planting director for about eighty-five churches from New Jersey to Maine. In this role, I meet with a lot of pastors and denominational leaders.

What makes me cry at times is the lack of passion and the defeated spirit I see in some. These guys are the walking wounded of the Kingdom of God. I once asked a pastor about vision and he said, "I have no vision for our church in this community." He was just living paycheck to paycheck, going through the motions, and punching the proverbial clock until retirement.

I'd rather die.

I realize how this happens and I grieve for those in this position, but isn't our God great enough to change us and rekindle the fire for the gospel we once had? I believe He is and that He's shouting to us that this is *exactly* His intent!

Remember Fonzie from the old *Happy Days* TV show? His motto was, "Live fast, die young, and leave a good looking corpse." I'm not suggesting this exactly, but wouldn't you rather go out in a blaze of glory, than punch the clock until retirement? I guess I'm saying, "Yes, they *could* fire you—but so what?" Is Matthew 6:33 true or isn't it? Is Jesus a liar or the personification of truth?! If He promises to take care of you when you put His kingdom above the will of a few stubborn bored, (oops, I mean board) members, He *means it*! So go for it pastor!

4. But I'm tired!

This is related to number 3, but it's not so much based on a fear of loss of income or employment as it is on the feeling of depression or emotional, spiritual, or physical fatigue. I get it! After the Worldwide Church of God transition, I actually was diagnosed with mild depression and was given prescription medication for about six months. During some of the transition, at least the early stages, my wife suffered from chronic fatigue syndrome and spent the better part of two years in bed. Believe me—*I get it*!

So you may need a sabbatical or an extended break before taking on a death and rebirth project. Scripture models this kind of Sabbath rest repeatedly for our benefit. But to paraphrase that old poem, "Rest if you must…but don't you quit!"14 Take a break, but come back and do what you *know* God is calling you to do. He'll empower and strengthen you. It's His work after all, isn't it?

5. Shouldn't I care for the sheep—even the ones who don't want to change?

The answer to this one is a firm "Yes and No." Seriously, sometimes the answer is yes because you can show them, from the Bible, the need for change in obedience to Christ. But when they are unwilling to consider it and will only hold back or create obstacles to change, you need to let them go.

This is a judgment call and one that must be directed by the Holy Spirit. But which is more important, having more people saved because you did what was necessary to reach them or the possibility of keeping a few disgruntled, grouchy sheep on board? In other words, if in doubt, opt for outreach and the Great Commission. Do you try to bring everyone along? Yes! But *never* at the expense of the lost!

6. But we've always done it this way and it worked before!

In the first-century church, preaching in synagogues was a very effective outreach strategy. Peter did it. Paul did, too. It was a natural starting point for church planting since the Jews and God-fearing Greeks would be the first to respond. After all, they had a foundation of truth from the Old Testament. It worked…until about 80 AD. At that point, Christians were excluded from that environment, as they are today. At that point, entering the synagogue, let alone preaching or sharing there would land you in jail, or perhaps result in martyrdom. My point is that what "always" worked, no longer worked.

Most pastors know this aspect of church history. Still, when it comes to having a service at a different time to reach more lost people, we will fight for the death to keep our 8:00 a.m. worship meeting, even though the average attendance is now only 10 (down from 100).

7. If God is sovereign, didn't He lead us to do what we've always done?

Again, this is related to objection number 6, but the answer is a firm "Maybe." I remember people at

Worldwide suggesting that God had given us all of Herbert W. Armstrong's teachings "for a reason." Well, the problem with that is, it would make God a heretic. No, God decidedly did *not* give us Armstrong's doctrine. He allowed us to have it, sure, but that's a far cry from tacit approval or divine determinism (apologies to my Calvinist friends).

But even *if* God gave you the prior strategy or structure, that doesn't mean He intended it to be a permanent installation. Just as with the synagogue outreach strategy, culture changes, therefore strategies must adjust. Calvinists—you'll love this part—God's sovereignty has already allowed Him to foresee this. Who knows? You could be reading this book right now to prepare for what He's already predestined for your church!

8. **If we lose people, won't we suffer financially? What if we go bankrupt?**

It's no secret; pastors count "nickels and noses" every week. Pastors know that if noses go down (attendance drops), nickels will surely drop (giving). So what do we do with that? We invest. Truthfully, if your church is reborn, you will likely grow and you'll end up with more income than you now have. In the short term, you'll have to say goodbye to some big givers and deal with the pain.

Could you go bankrupt? I suppose, but would that be the end of the world? What if you had to meet in rented space or homes for a while? You could, you know. What if you had to take a part-time job? You could you know—thousands of pastors have and still do. But, if this is of God and you reach more lost people, eventually, things will turn around.

During times of transition I've had to do several things to support myself and my churches. I've painted houses, driven a cab, worked security jobs (third shift even—yuck!), sold copiers, and more. I used to joke that I should make business cards which say, "Joel Rissinger, AFAB (Anything for a Buck)." But is it worth it? A million times—*yes*!

9. Isn't this "Crucify Your Church" thing just another fad?

I wish! As I write this, I'm not sure anyone will actually read it, let alone do it. But let me dream for a moment. If this idea takes off, it won't be a fad. It will be a move of the Holy Spirit. Why? Because only the Holy Spirit could make something so radical become popular. Isn't that the history of Christianity, by the way? You bet it is!

With all books on church health and growth, I ask the same question: Is it biblical? If yes, fad or not, I'm going to do it. You should ask the same question of this book.

10. Shouldn't we just go slowly? If we change too fast, we'll fall apart or we'll be shut down!

What is the point of slowness? Too often it is granted to appease Christians who have not put forth the effort to evaluate the biblical and Spirit led nature of a given change. How is this different from a wife who gives her husband money so he can buy booze and then complains that she lives in an alcoholic household? In other words, we enable bad attitudes and then grieve their existence.

I say move as quickly as possible and love them all, while obeying Jesus. If the Lord told you to stop watching pornography, would you say, "Okay, Lord, but can I just slowly ease out of it by watching it twice a day instead of three times first?" I hope not. Change that's scriptural and for the sake of the growth of Christ's Bride should be embraced immediately, if not sooner. Will some leave? You bet! Will more new people come? Always! Is it worth it? Eternally!

Chapter 11

Hospice Care

Resurrection. There is perhaps no more powerful event in all of scripture. Bringing the dead back to life is the essence of Christ's Lordship. In fact, it is the only sign Jesus gave of His Messiahship (Matthew 12:39). So, at least until the second coming, it is rare and yet earth-shatteringly significant when it occurs!

Sadly, I believe this is profoundly true of churches. To have even a chance at revival, we have to crucify the old paradigms and approaches—yes, we in essence kill the church we serve. And, while doing that is hard enough, we must at the same time recognize that bringing it back from the dead may be the hardest and most supernaturally dependent part of the process.

Truth is—many never revive. Statistics suggest that most partially reform, split, or even dissolve, but that very few are truly reborn. Unfortunately, many aren't willing to follow the principles of this book as a group and thus they die. So, before we embark on this church crucifixion journey, we have to prepare for the possibility that our church may lie in the grave till our Savior returns.

Are you ready for that?

I call this the "Church Hospice Care" principle. When we know that a loved one's time has come, we often call on those amazing and incredibly loving hospice care nurses. There's a special place in heaven for those who gently help people peacefully transfer from this life to the next. They provide care, medicine, and comfort to grieving family members. They are ministering servants at one of life's most crucial times. My point is that just as individuals and families need hope, so do dying churches.

My friend and mentor, Paul Hubley, District Executive Minister for Converge Northeast is a church hospice care expert. Several times, I've seen him help a church recognize that it was time to close up shop and that, while they should celebrate a eulogy of their past, the likelihood (or even wisdom) of attempting a resurrection was minimal. Lack of leadership, resources, or just vision for new birth sometimes makes death a funeral celebration of sorts, and in essence a burial—the best choice.

Paul often explains that just as a loved one leaves his or her family an inheritance, a dying church can leave financial resources to another church or churches that will be born or planted as a result of their generosity. This brings new life to the Kingdom through the passing of a single local church.

Clearly, this is a delicate, difficult ministry, but Paul Hubley and other apostolic leaders like him do it well, and for God's glory. People are helped to find new church homes, resources are used for kingdom purposes, and life goes on. You see, people like Paul know that to prolong life through artificial means would only prolong suffering and thus delay the use of church resources elsewhere. Rather than promoting the "holy huddle" of what is often just a handful of older people in a massive, otherwise empty building, they need to accept the reality of the situation and move on.

Is this the situation your church is in? Only God can answer that, but here are some key questions which may help:

1. Do you have leadership to cast a new, godly vision?
2. Do you have the manpower and physical energy to reach out to your community?
3. Are you financially sound so as to avoid bankruptcy?
4. If you do nothing, will the general trend and direction lead to success over dissolution?

If you've answered "No" to even one of those questions, "church hospice care" is worth prayerful consideration. Do you have a denominational or apostolic leader you can turn to for guidance in this decision? Is this person someone who will make sure your property and other assets can help plant a new church? Will he help your remaining members find other healthy churches? Seek their guidance.

And if your church is a candidate for hospice, let me make one other suggestion: Please help give birth to a new church! As a church planter and a coach to others who do this very challenging ministry, I can tell you that the biggest need we have is CASH! I know, you wanted me to say something spiritual like prayer or emotional support or Christmas cards—but CASH is King for new churches folks. That's just the way it is.

So if churches who need to close would donate buildings, land, and other resources, church plants like mine would be blessed. Some churches even intentionally bond with new planters to transition from one body and leadership structure to another. I've seen this work successfully where a congregation has dwindled in size to a small handful and then deeds their building to a new core group to launch a brand new congregation. Christ is honored in this kind of cooperative effort. Could your church be a candidate for such a venture?

Chapter 12

Born Again—Born Anew— Born from Above!

Nothing is more joyful than new birth. Holding a newborn baby can melt all the world's evil into nothingness, just like that. Even the pain and stress of childbirth is suddenly forgotten.

My son's birth was like that. After ten hours of full minute contractions which were three minutes apart (or shorter) minutes apart, duress on the baby had affected his heart rate and almost forced a C-section. Still, when it was over, I watched my wife holding our baby and actually heard her say, "You know, that wasn't so bad."

Wow!

Spiritual rebirth is even more dramatic and inspiring. I've often told people—you can forget a ton of garbage you've faced over several weeks time by watching just one lost soul cross the line of faith. Even the angels in heaven celebrate more for just one sinner who repents, than for the rest of us who've "been there, done that."

So what do you suppose happens in the heavens when an entire church chooses to "die to self in order to live for God?" Par-tay! One massive, mind-blowing party—that's what happens! And I believe we should join in the celebration!

When a church faces all the challenges outlined in this book and is fully reborn, a celebration is necessary. People need to be reinforced and assured of the tremendous hope their decisions have enabled. Other churches and friends need the witness this occasion brings. It's a testimony to the saving grace and power of Almighty God. This celebration should honor and recognize the goodness of the past, while clearly recognizing the fresh, clean, resurrected start. Key leaders—formal and informal in their positions of influence—should be recognized. It's a *big* deal, and rightly so!

On the heels of this supernaturally supported party, move forward quickly. Use the joyous momentum to tackle the challenge of starting over. Make sure you're committed to growing and multiplying. Hold fast to the doctrinal and missional purposes we've discussed thus far. And as you go, here are some cautions:

- **Watch out for zombies.** Zombies are what sci-fi writers call "the living dead," an oxymoron for sure. These are sad, dead creatures, but they don't know it. They are thus empowered to walk around, wreaking havoc.

  In church life, zombies come in several forms following a church death, burial, and resurrection. Zombies can be ministries that escaped the review of leaders during the transformation process. They "didn't get the memo" about their demise and refuse to go away. They often have leaders who have either willfully, ignorantly, or unintentionally missed the new direction.

  Our tendency, when encountering these specters of past church life, is to ignore them. Basically, we reason that they will eventually go away or die of attrition. But you see, that's the problem with zombies—they refuse to die. They need firm, loving, and unrelenting direction from senior staff members. Often, this will be blunt and forceful in nature, or else these zombies will continue to wander the streets and alleys of your new church, wreaking havoc along the way. You *must* face them and defeat them, once and for all.

  After one of our church transitions, we encountered several zombies. In one case, two or three of our leaders were running a Bible study which didn't fit into the discipleship strategy we had agreed on for the new church. The primary leader had refused to go through a training program required for all leaders, yet he continued to lead this study anyway. Finally, I encountered them meeting during services in the fellowship area directly in defiance of our senior leadership. We ultimately had no choice but to close it down and ask the rebel leaders to either cease and desist or find another place of worship.

Some found this cruel. Yet, I believe this kind of swift and direct action is often necessary. One week before we shut down the zombie study, a new believer asked us, "What is that study group about? They don't seem to fit what I was told about small groups at this church. Besides they don't seem happy about things here…are they okay?"

Clearly, damage was being done—and to baby Christians no less! Just like those B-level horror movies, if you let the zombies alone, they'll multiply and overrun your church, leaving death and destruction in their wake.

- **Move forward, but don't throw the baby out with the bathwater.** Just because you did something before, doesn't mean it's bad *per se*. If it supports your new vision—do it! This is the converse of my last zombie point. In other words, we're not doing new things just for the sake of newness, they simply must be based on God's dictum and call. If the old program or ministry works—just do it, but in a new, fresh way.

- **Let people grieve, but with hope.** In 1 Thessalonians 4, Paul tells the saints that they should not grieve like the rest of the world, that is, grieving without hope (verses 16–17). To crucify a church, give birth to a new one, and then move on without acknowledging the loss, is impossible. Still, shepherds must remind the grieving flock that there's a new beginning and an exciting future ahead. It's a fine line. An almost surgically precise level of pastoral care is needed, allowing grief, while casting vision for a future filled with hope. Tough or not, it *must* be done or the pain will increase and destruction will result.

- **When people leave, keep moving forward and don't look back.** The most painful experience a shepherd has is when sheep flee the pen. The temptation is to drop everything and chase them—pleading with them to return to the fold. At these times, we second guess everything and sometimes put the new direction on hold, so as to stop the bleeding and avoid losing more sheep. This is a huge mistake!

I've even had other members or leaders quote Luke 15, using the lost sheep parable to shove me out of the gate to "leave the ninety-nine in search of the one" who had left. Without an exegesis of the parable, I'll simply say that the point of the entire chapter is that lost people matter to God. This is something Bill Hybels has pointed out for years. Luke 15 is not about stubborn, believing sheep who church-hop when things aren't going their way. It's about unbelievers who matter to God! Regardless, we must resist the urge to chase those who reject the new church.

"Remember," one pastor friend of mine would often say, "they're Christ's sheep anyway and He loves them and will care for them far better than we ever could." Your new, reborn church needs you focused and at the helm. When sheep flee, *let them go!*

- **Tell the world!** Church rebirth is a huge deal. Advertise it, do mailings and press releases, give interviews—all of the above! Let the unchurched world know about what God is doing—for His name's sake. Regeneration is working—that's Good News (pardon the pun)!

If you do it right, you'll be surprised at how many new folks will show up just to see what's going on. We've always tried to develop and maintain a good relationship with local media, print, TV, and radio. We email press releases regularly and it's amazing how often we get published. This results in free advertising for the church. If you survive a death and rebirth—use the press to publish something good for a change!

- **Be fruitful and multiply.** Jesus called the first disciples, telling them that their new identity was to be "fishers of men." Multiplying new disciples is the *primary* role of *every believer*. I also believe this is true of every church. A healthy church will always multiply. This may be new worship sites and campuses, new churches, or both—but she *cannot* remain stagnant or only build herself up. When this happens, her death is inevitable. Make sure that your vision and goals include the birth of new churches—constantly remaining fresh in the process.

Conclusion

It's time for honesty in the face of impending disaster. Every analyst agrees, the church in America is dying. Islam is the fastest growing religion in our country and, rather than saving souls, Christian leaders are organizing shuffleboard games on the deck of the Titanic. Working harder, or simply using failed programs more vigorously isn't the answer. Nor is the answer to do nothing, while we watch our own demise. Instead, we need to accept the reality of the state of the modern church. We need to reject the façade of renewal. We need to understand that death to self is the essence of modern Christianity. Then, we have to crucify the doctrinal, structural, visional, missional, and nominal nature of our church such that Jesus can resurrect it in newness of life!

Are you willing to face this? Is your local church willing to die to self in order to truly *live* for God?

I pray that the answer to that question is a resounding "Yes!"

About the Author

Pastor Joel L. Rissinger and his wife Karen have been married for more than twenty-five years and have two children, David, age 23, and Shelly, age 21. Pastor Joel is the lead and founding pastor of Mill Pond Church in Newington, Connecticut. Mill Pond started with fifteen people, mostly teens, in the Rissinger's living room. Three years later, Mill Pond has about 200 regular attendees in two worship locations.

Pastor Joel has been in fulltime ministry since 1992. In this capacity, he has led several congregations through major transitions prior to planting Mill Pond Church in 2007. This included leading two congregations out of doctrinal heresy as part of the Worldwide Church of God. Later, he would help take a 118-year-old church from an inwardly focused, program-centered approach, to a purpose-driven philosophy, and ultimately a merger with two other local churches.

In addition to his pastoral duties, Pastor Joel is the Director of Church Multiplication for Converge Northeast

(Baptist General Conference), serves as the chaplain for The ABC Women's Center of Middletown, Connecticut; is the New England Regional Coordinator for The Antioch School of Church Planting and Leadership Development, and is a seminar presenter for Life Innovations, Inc., and their popular Prepare-Enrich marriage counseling program.

Pastor Joel has a BA in theology from Ambassador University, as well as MAs in both religion and religious education from Liberty University. He is currently pursuing a D.Min. from the Antioch School in Ames, Iowa.

Appendix 1.

Constitution of Mill Pond Church, Inc.

ARTICLE ONE

Section 1. Organization

The organization is named **Mill Pond Church, Inc.** and was first incorporated as Mill Pond Church, Inc., on January 4, 2007.

Section 2. Offices

The principal office of **Mill Pond Church, Inc.** hereinafter referred to as the Corporation, shall be located at the address set forth in the Articles of Incorporation. The Corporation may have such offices, either within or without the State of Incorporation, as the board of Trustees may determine.

Section 3. Corporation

This Corporation is organized exclusively for charitable, religious and educational purposes, including for such purposes, the making of distributions to organizations that qualify as exempt organizations under section 501(c)3 of the Internal Revenue Code, or the corresponding section of any future federal tax code.

No part of the net earnings of the Corporation shall inure to the benefits of or be distributable to its members, Trustees, officers, or other private persons, except that the Corporation shall be authorized and empowered to pay reasonable compensation for services rendered and to make payments and distributions in furtherance of the purposes set forth in the above paragraph.

Not withstanding any other provisions of these articles, the Corporation shall not carry on any other activities not permitted to be carried on (a) by a corporation exempt from Federal income tax under section 501(c)3 of the Internal Revenue Code, or the corresponding section of any future federal tax code, or (b) by a corporation, contributions to which are deductible under section 170(c)(2) of the Internal Revenue Code, or corresponding section of any future federal tax code. No substantial part of the activities of this corporation shall be the carrying on of propaganda, or otherwise attempting to influence legislation except as otherwise provided by Section 501(h) of the Internal Revenue Code, and this corporation shall not participate in, or intervene in (including the publishing or distribution of statements), any political campaign on behalf of, or in opposition to, any candidate for public office.

Section 4. Dissolution

Upon the dissolution of the Corporation, assets shall be distributed for one or more exempt purposes within the meaning of section 501(c)3 of the Internal Revenue Code, or the corresponding section of any future federal tax code, or shall be distributed to the federal government or to a state or local government for public purpose. Any such assets not so disposed of shall be disposed of by a Court of Competent Jurisdiction of the county in which the principal office of the Corporation is then located, exclusively for such purposes or to such organization or organizations, as said Court shall determine, which are organized and operated exclusively for such purposes. Furthermore, should conditions arise when, for any reason, the Church ceases to function, the Church property shall be transferred to the Northeast Baptist Conference unless otherwise stated by the congregation provided the Conference is a tax exempt organization within the meaning of Section 501(c) (3) of the Internal Revenue Code.

Section 5. Affiliation

The Church will be affiliated with the Northeast Baptist Conference and the Baptist General Conference.

ARTICLE TWO

AFFIRMATION OF FAITH

(Adopted by the Baptist General Conference in 1951, reaffirmed in 1990 and amended in 1998.)

1. The Word of God: We believe that the Bible is the Word of God, fully inspired and without error in the original manu- scripts, written under the inspiration of the Holy Spirit, and that it has supreme authority in all matters of faith and conduct.

2. The Trinity: We believe that there is one living and true God, eternally existing in three persons, that these are equal in every divine perfection, and that they execute distinct but harmonious offices in the work of creation, providence and redemption.

3. God the Father: We believe in God, the Father, an infinite, personal spirit, perfect in holiness, wisdom, power and love. We believe that He concerns Himself mercifully in the affairs

of each person, that He hears and answers prayer, and that He saves from sin and death all who come to Him through Jesus Christ.

4. Jesus Christ: We believe in Jesus Christ, God's only begotten Son, conceived by the Holy Spirit. We believe in His virgin birth, sinless life, miracles and teachings. We believe in His substitutionary atoning death, bodily resurrection, ascension into heaven, perpetual intercession for His people, and personal visible return to earth.

5. The Holy Spirit: We believe in the Holy Spirit who came forth from the Father and Son to convict the world of sin, righteousness, and judgment, and to regenerate, sanctify, and empower all who believe in Jesus Christ. We believe that the Holy Spirit indwells every believer in Christ, and that He is an abiding helper, teacher and guide.

6. Regeneration: We believe that all people are sinners by nature and by choice and are, therefore, under condemnation. We believe that those who repent of their sins and trust in Jesus Christ as Savior are regenerated by the Holy Spirit.

7. The Church: We believe in the universal church, a living spiritual body of which Christ is the head and all regenerated persons are members.

We believe in the local church, consisting of a company of believers in Jesus Christ, baptized on a credible profession of faith, and associated for worship, work and fellowship. We believe that God has laid upon the members of the local church the primary task of giving the gospel of Jesus Christ to a lost world.

8. Christian Conduct: We believe that Christians should live for the glory of God and the well-being of others; that their conduct should be blameless before the world; that they should be faithful stewards of their possessions; and that they should seek to realize for themselves and others the full stature of maturity in Christ.

9. The Ordinances: We believe that the Lord Jesus Christ has committed two ordinances to the local church: baptism and the Lord's Supper. We believe that Christian baptism is the immersion of a believer in water into the name of the triune God. We believe that the Lord's Supper was instituted by Christ for commemoration of His death. We believe that these

two ordinances should be observed and administered until the return of the Lord Jesus Christ.

10. Religious Liberty: We believe that every human being has direct relations with God, and is responsible to God alone in all matters of faith; that each church is independent and must be free from interference by any ecclesiastical or political authority; that therefore Church and State must be kept separate as having different functions, each fulfilling its duties free from dictation or patronage of the other.

11. Church Cooperation: We believe that local churches can best promote the cause of Jesus Christ by cooperating with one another in a denominational organization. Such an organization, whether it is the Conference or a district conference, exists and functions by the will of the churches. Cooperation in a conference is voluntary and may be terminated at any time. Churches may likewise cooperate with interdenominational fellowships on a voluntary basis.

12. The Last Things: We believe in the personal and visible return of the Lord Jesus Christ to earth and the establishment of His kingdom. We believe in the resurrection of the body, the final judgment, the eternal felicity of the righteous, and the endless suffering of the wicked.

ARTICLE THREE

Section 1. Mission

Mill Pond Church exists to reach people, help bring them to a relationship with Jesus Christ and then assist them as He transforms their lives.

Section 2. Vision

Mill Pond Church is committed to helping hundreds of people:

Connect in meaningful relationships.

Celebrate God in regular worship.

Cooperate with others in service to church and community.

Communicate the good news about Jesus Christ.

Cultivate a life that is truly fulfilling by following Jesus daily.

Section 3. Values

We value:

* Relationships over religion.

* Faith over formality.

* Message over method.

* Truth over tradition.

* People...we value relationships and the creation of new ones between people of all ages, races, ethnicities, economic backgrounds, etc.

* The Bible as the revealed word of God. It's the basis of all we teach and do.

* Generosity—in our lives, in our church, and in our global community.

* God's purposes—Worship, Real Fellowship/Relationships, Spiritual Maturity, Service/Ministry, and Evangelism. The purposes of God create a plan for living. Thus, we believe the 5 purposes above lead us to:

—Worship in a celebrating, reflective, and effective manner every day.

—Walk our spiritual path with others—no one should travel alone.

—Work at spiritual maturity.

—Welcome opportunities to serve. Every member is a minister.

—Witness. We're all on mission with God, helping others come to Him.

ARTICLE FOUR

Section 1. Membership

Members shall be all people, (16 years and older for voting members), who have been born-again in Christ, who have been baptized, by immersion, at Mill Pond Church or a church of like faith, and have completed and are in agreement with the basic membership CLASS 101. Members' voting responsibilities are described in Article nine, sub-section three.

Section 2. Membership Removal & Reinstatement

Members can be removed from Mill Pond Church by the Senior Pastor (or his designee) for the following reasons:

- Death
- Transfer of membership
- Church discipline (see article eight, section one)
- Personal request
- Inactivity

Members can be reinstated at the discretion of the Senior Pastor, or his designees.

ARTICLE FIVE

Section 1. The Government

The Senior Pastor, the Board of Elders, the Board of Trustees and the Congregation govern Mill Pond Church. The Senior Pastor and staff are responsible for all day-to-day operations of the church. The staff reports to the Senior Pastor (or his designee). The Board of Elders provides spiritual oversight, guidance, prayer and general support to the body. The Board of Trustees is responsible for the management of the Corporation and major financial decisions. The Congregation is responsible to vote on the selection of a new Senior Pastor, to approve or reject the purchase or disposition of property and/or buildings or to change or amend the constitution.

Section 2. Senior Pastor/President of the Corporation

Because Mill Pond Church has two complimentary branches – the Spiritual Body and the legal Corporation, the Senior Pastor serves a dual role. The Senior Pastor is responsible for the spiritual direction of the body and the legal mandate to lead the legal Corporation. The responsibilities of the Senior Pastor/President include but are not limited to:

Sub-section 1. Responsibilities as Senior Pastor

- Provide Biblical vision and direction for the body

- Define and communicate the purpose of the church
- Oversee all day-to-day operation of ministry
- Staff the church as needed for healthy growth
- Review and determine all staff and salaries

Sub-section 2. Responsibilities as President of Corporation

- Serve as ex-officio member of all standing groups
- Serve as chair for all committees (or have designee)
- Select Trustees (with Elder approval)
- Hire, direct, or dismiss church staff as needed.
- May execute, with the approval of the Trustees, in the name of the Corporation all deeds, leases, loans, bonds and contracts
- Develop and submit budgets to the Trustees.

Section 3. Board of Elders

The Board of Elders, consists of at least three elders, serves the Senior Pastor as advisors, the congregation as spiritual overseers, helps provide spiritual direction and meets on a regular basis. If at any time the number of elders dips below three, the Senior Pastor may choose to select other Pastors/ elders from sister churches to constitute the minimum requirement. If Mill Pond Church later ordains additional elders the replacements from the other churches will be immediately dismissed. Elders are to help create a positive spiritual climate within the church body. Elders serve as shepherds. Elders should be available to the Pastor (and staff) to assist in ministry functions as needed. Elders must meet the requirements set forth in 1 Timothy 3:1-13, Titus 1:6-9. Their calling is life-long and therefore, must be taken very seriously.

Sub-section 1. Additional Functions

- Provide a prayer shield for the Pastoral team and church
- Defend, protect and support the integrity of the Pastoral team and church
- Pray for and lay hands on the sick
- Mediate disputes within the church body
- Ordain other Elders, Pastors and Deacons
- Confirm or reject Pastoral appointments to Trustees
- Initiate investigation and potential discipline of Senior Pastor
- Offer review of Senior Pastor to Trustees
- Participate, when appropriate, in matters of discipline

Sub-section 2. Nomination and Approval

Elders are nominated by the Elders and approved by a two-thirds vote of the existing Board of Elders. The congregation is encouraged to recommend suggestions for possible Elder candidates. Elders may serve as long as they are able and as long as they continue to meet the Biblical requirements. Elders may take a leave of absence of up to, but not exceeding, one year with written, prior approval of the Elder Board.

Sub-section 3. Dismissal from the Board and Reinstatement

After seeking wise counsel from at least two other Elders/ Pastors, the Senior Pastor may dismiss an Elder from the Board, not to exceed a rate of one per twelve months (unless multiple Elders or their spouses exhibit moral or ethical failure). Existing Elders are not required to approve the Senior Pastor's dismissal of an Elder. An Elder may be reinstated to the Board with the approval of the Senior Pastor and by a two-thirds vote of existing Board of Elders.

Sub-section 4. Removal

Concerns from the congregation against an Elder must meet biblical guidelines found in Matthew 18 and 1 Timothy 5:19-21. The Elder Board will review all concerns in detail. If an Elder is unable to fulfill his role because he no longer meets the biblical qualifications, the Elder Board will require them to step down.

Sub-section 5. Reinstatement

Reinstatement of an Elder will be reviewed on a case-by-case basis by the Senior Pastor and the Board of Elders.

Section 4. Board of Trustees

Sub-section 1. General Powers

The major financial and operational affairs of the church will be governed by the Board of Trustees, hereinafter referred to as the Trustees, whose members shall have fiduciary responsibility to the corporation. As President of the Corporation, the Senior Pastor (or his designee) will act as Chairman of the Trustees.

Sub-section 2. Appointment, Number, Term and Qualifications

The Board of Trustees shall number at least three members and will consist of the Treasurer, other officers of the Corporation, certain Elders and/or other members chosen by the Senior Pastor and approved by a majority vote of the Elders. The term of the office of Trustee shall continue until said Trustee resigns from office or church membership, dies or is removed. Trustees must be members in good standing for at least one year (reviewed on a case-by-case basis) and display a mature Christian walk and testimony.

Sub-section 3. Dismissal

After seeking wise council, the Pastor may dismiss a Trustee from the board (not to exceed one per twelve months, unless in the case of multiple moral/ethical failures). Existing Trustees or Elders are not required to approve dismissal by the Senior Pastor of a Trustee.

Sub-section 4. Functions

- The Trustees oversee the provision and management of facilities needed by the church body. They will also coordinate any construction projects that require a loan or mortgage.
- The Trustees have the authority to buy and sell land or buildings (with congregational approval); secure leases and borrow money.
- Determine Senior Pastor's salary and benefits with recommendations from Pastoral Annual Review.

In order to provide for the physical needs of the church body, the Trustees have available to them 100% of all unrestricted monies in checking and saving accounts, CD's or other investment accounts. Trustees have the authority to approve or reject budgets. The Senior Pastor has a discretionary one-time spending cap of five thousand dollars over a 30 day period (with treasurer approval). All spending beyond that limit requires Trustee Board approval. Only officers of the Corporation may sign checks.

Sub-section 5. Meetings

A Trustee meeting will take place at least six times per year. The President of the Corporation will act as chair and a secretary will be appointed to take minutes.

If the President is not available, the Corporation vice-president or secretary will act on his behalf. The meeting location will be announced at least one-week prior and Trustees must attend. A simple-majority of Trustees will constitute a quorum. A simple majority will pass a motion unless otherwise noted by this constitution.

Section 5. The Congregation

Sub-section 1. General Authority to Select a New Senior Pastor

Should the need arise to select a new Senior Pastor; the congregation is responsible for the approval. Two methods are provided in the selection process.

Sub-section 2. Departing Pastor Participates in Process

If the Pastor is in good standing with the church and is removing himself for any reason except failure to meet biblical or moral standards described herein, the following will constitute the selection process for his replacement:

The Senior Pastor may choose a short list of candidates. The first candidate is to speak during three or more regularly scheduled services and will be available to the congregation for questions. The Senior Pastor will then call a business meeting of the church with at least fourteen days prior notice. During the meeting, the congregation will vote by ballot. The Trustees and Elders are to tally and certify the votes. With a minimum 80 percent vote, the candidate will be accepted. If that candidate fails, the second candidate will repeat the process.

Sub-section 3. Congregational Process without Departing Pastor's Participation (Pastoral Selection Committee)

If the Senior Pastor is removed, deceased, cannot or will not participate in the selection process, the following shall be the selection process:

The Board of Elders will select an Interim Pastor until a permanent replacement is found. They will then conduct a search and present a short list of candidates to the congregation. The first candidate is to speak during three or more regularly scheduled services and will be available to the congregation for questions. The Elders will then call a business meeting of the church with at least fourteen days prior notice. During the meeting, the congregation will vote by ballot. The Trustees and Elders are to tally and certify the votes. With a minimum 80 percent vote, the candidate will be accepted. If that candidate fails, the second candidate will repeat the process, etc., until a new Senior Pastor is ratified.

During the transition time, the Elders will have responsibility for oversight of the church body. If an Interim Pastor has not yet been named or is unavailable, they will provide pulpit supply as needed. The Interim Pastor, existing staff and the Trustees are responsible for day-to-day church operations including all duties of the Senior Pastor described herein. Once a new Senior Pastor is selected, he will be appointed as President of the Corporation and will have full authority to select and replace existing staff if he chooses. Any existing staff designated for replacement or termination will be given at least thirty days notice and at least two weeks of severance pay for each complete year of service (example three complete years of service equals six weeks of severance pay).

ARTICLE SIX

Deacons

Deacons will be individuals who meet the biblical qualifications found in 1 Timothy 3:8-13. Deacons are responsible for the physical needs of the church body. Their spouses must meet the biblical qualifications as found in 1 Timothy 3:11.

Sub-section 1. Election of Deacons

The Elder Board will accept nominations from the congregation all who are members in good standing. These men will be considered by the Elders, and will be tested according to Scripture to verify that they meet the biblical qualifications. If approved, the Elders will present them to the congregation for commissioning.

Sub-section 2. Additional Functions

- Minister to widows, orphans and the poor
- Provide direct care to families not connected to small groups
- Help identify physical and spiritual needs within the body
- Oversee the administration of Baptism and Communion
- Assist Senior Pastor, Elders and/or Staff when called on

Sub-section 3. Removal of Deacons

Concerns from the congregation against a Deacon must meet biblical guidelines found in Matthew 18 and 1 Timothy 5:19-21. The Elder Board will review all concerns in detail. If a Deacon unable to fulfill his role because he no longer meets the biblical qualifications, the Elder Board will require him to step down.

Sub-section 4. Reinstatement of Deacons

If a former Deacon, who was removed, has repented and currently meets the biblical qualifications, he may ask to be reinstated by the Elder Board and congregation. He would then be required to go through the nomination and testing process again.

ARTICLE SEVEN

Officers of the Corporation

Officers of the Corporation shall be as follows - President, Vice-President, and Treasurer. Officers must be members in good standing for at least one year (reviewed on a case-by-case basis) and display a mature Christian walk and testimony. Appointment of an officer is the responsibility of the President with majority approval by the Board of Elders. If the President is unable to appoint, the Trustees will act on his behalf and the Elders must approve this appointment by a majority vote. Officers shall serve without term limits. The President of the Corporation may remove and replace officers with majority support by the Board of Elders.

ARTICLE EIGHT

Church Discipline

Section 1. Disciplining Members
Only church members may be disciplined in accordance with Matthew 18:15-17.

Section 2. Disciplining the Senior Pastor
Should the Senior Pastor demonstrate moral, ethical or theological practices, which the Elders believe may require personal change or discipline, they shall first contact the Senior Pastor. If the conduct continues, they may then contact the NBC District Executive Minister. The DEM may be asked to investigate. Following his investigation, he may recommend to the Board of Elders *no action, discipline or removal.* The DEM has no authority except that given to him by the Elders and then only as is allowed by this constitution. Removal requires a majority vote by the Board of Elders.

ARTICLE NINE

Meetings

Sub-section 1. Public Worship

The congregation shall meet each weekend for worship.

   a. Communion. The Lord's Supper shall be observed at least once a quarter.
   b. Baptism. Baptisms will be performed as often as needed, at the discretion of the Senior Pastor and/or staff.

Sub-section 2. Congregational Meetings

There will be at least one congregational meeting per year, as close to the beginning of the fiscal year as possible, with other meetings as needed. The meeting may occur during morning worship or at another time. Meetings may be open or closed to members only at the discretion of the Senior Pastor and the Elders. Notice of such meetings shall be posted and announced at least two weeks in advance.

Sub-section 3. Voting & Quorums

For a members meeting called to address a voting requirement, a quorum is defined as 20% of the active membership of Mill Pond Church. Voting items include:

- Amendments/Changes to Constitution
- Acquisition or disposition of real property
- Calling a new Senior Pastor

A simple majority is required to pass motions by the congregation, unless otherwise stated in this constitution.

ARTICLE TEN

Amending the Constitution

This constitution may be altered, modified or repealed by a majority vote of the Board of Elders and the Board of Trustees. The Congregation must also approve with a majority vote. Written, public notice must be given along with the proposal for alteration at least two weeks prior to meeting and vote.

ARTICLE ELEVEN

Interpretation

The interpretation of this constitution and in all matters not addressed by this constitution but which affect Mill Pond Church will be determined by the Board of Elders and the Board of Trustees. Their combined, majority vote on interpretation will have final authority.

Appendix ii

Note: This article appeared in our church newsletter during our transition toward a more Elder-led structure. It is reprinted here for clarity and/or for use as you see fit...

Just What IS an Elder Anyway?
...A Study Guide

What is an Elder? To answer this question, we need to start at the very beginning of the New Testament Church era. But first, perhaps we should quickly look at what an Elder is NOT. A Biblical Church Elder is NOT:

- An elderly or "older" man per se.
- Someone "elected" to that office by church members.
- Someone "more important" than others.
- Someone who likes to "give orders."
- Someone who has, "climbed the ladder" as a deacon, and has "earned the title," etc.

An Elder is the Bible was never one who thought he wanted more power or influence and therefore pursued the office for that reason. He was never one who could study or do good works such that he'd be accepted in that office. He had to meet criteria that only God could establish and enable him to attain. In our context, he had to have the right S.H.A.P.E. for this office, and he had to have the right moral character and reputation too. As Jesus demonstrated, Elders are servants who "wash the feet" of those they lead and serve.

Historical Background

Actually, the first Elders were the early Apostles. Just as we understand the church to have "Circles of Commitment" today, the people living at the time of Jesus could be characterized as belonging to the "Community" (all those living in Judea and the towns where Jesus taught), the "Crowd" (such as 5,000 fed on one occasion), the "Congregation" (consisting of the 120 following Jesus as of Pentecost circa 33 AD), the "Committed" (as were the 70 who were sent out on a missions trip prior to the end of Jesus' earthly ministry), and the "Core" (the 12). Jesus also had what we might call an "inner circle," almost like a group of staff members or best friends who were closer to him than anyone else (James, Peter, and John).

Apparently, Jesus chose the 12 based on his knowledge of their personalities, their talents, and what would ultimately become their spiritual gifts. It was his desire to eventually give them authority (Matthew 16:17-19), as well as a calling to care for his followers (John 21:12-17), and a call to reach the lost (Matthew 28:19-20, Mark 1:17, etc.). After Jesus' death, resurrection, and ascension to heaven, the 12 understood that they were to lead as a group and acted quickly to replace Judas, after suicide, to keep the leadership team intact (Acts 1:13-26). The basic concept of a plurality of Elders acting as a team comes from the original Apostles.

The book of Acts as well as the record of early church history shows that the oversight of the church shifted from the Apostles (the 12) to groups of Elders in each local church. This shift occurred for four primary reasons:

1. The original 12 Apostles eventually died (John 21:18-19).
2. The church spread to many regions outside of Judea (Acts 1:8).
3. The ministry of Paul called for the naming of Elders in every town (Titus 1:5).
4. Even the original Apostles considered themselves Elders in a primary sense (see 2 Peter 5:1).

These Elders had oversight (Acts 20:17-31, Hebrews 13:17) and the authority to do several things:

- Lead and protect the flock (1 Timothy 5:17, etc.).
- Teach (1 Timothy 3:2).
- To lay on hands for ordination (Acts 6, 1 Timothy 4:14).
- Pray for and anoint the sick (James 5:14).
- Determine membership status (1 Corinthians 5:4-5).
- Correct and rebuke those caught in sin (1 Timothy 4:1-2).
- Restore people to membership (2 Corinthians 2:1-11)
- Equip the saints for works of ministry (Ephesians 4:11-16).

Qualifications

The qualifications for being called to the office of Elder are found in 1 Timothy 3 and Titus 1. Before listing them, it is important to note that nowhere in Scripture do we see any precedent for "terms of office" for Elders. These responsibilities, because they were based so heavily on gifting as well as moral example, were never considered temporary. While we can't dispute the wisdom in giving people a break from certain responsibilities in line with a sabbatical or Sabbath rest, the idea that one would CEASE from being an Elder during such a rest is clearly not found in Scripture. In fact, who is man that he should attempt to nullify what God has ordained based on some arbitrary policy?

This is important to understand when looking at the naming of Elders. While the congregation may help discern and affirm through the Holy Spirit, those who seem to meet the following criteria, it must be understood that God through the existing leadership, (Elders and Deacons), will ordain or finally place them in office (Acts 6:1-6, 1 Timothy 4:14, etc.). In a congregationally governed church, the members could certainly work with the other Elders or deacons to remove an Elder who ceased to meet the criteria found in scripture (Matthew 18:15-18, 1 Timothy 5:19-20, and more). If all the Elders became corrupt, one possibility might be to use other pastors or leaders from within the BGC or other local churches to act as moderators of a dispute. Still, while in office, Elders should be allowed to lead as Biblically mandated (Romans 12:8 and others).

Here is a summary of the biblical qualifications of an Elder as found in 1 Timothy 3 and Titus 1:

- ❖ A man, (there are no female Elders)
- ❖ A blameless reputation

❖ Not self-willed.

❖ Soberv

❖ Hospitable.

❖ Not abusing alcohol/drugs.

❖ Not easily angered—not a "hothead."

❖ Loves the good in people and sees it.

❖ One who doesn't like to fight or argue.

❖ A gifted leader in his home.

❖ Holy/Called and "Set Apart."

❖ Will stand against heresy.

❖ Good reputation with unbelievers.

❖ A heart or desire to do good.

❖ *Spiritually* bound to only one woman.

❖ Diligent as a just leader.

❖ A good moral example.

❖ Gifted to teach.

❖ Not violent or abusive.

❖ Not greedy.

❖ Patient.

❖ Not covetous of others power, etc.

❖ A mature Christian.

❖ Balanced and given to moderation.

❖ Knows the Word.

Even these criteria speak to God's desire that these men should lead, oversee, and protect the congregation. The idea that they should only "teach and pray" while other "elected" church officials rule and make the churches business decisions, etc., is clearly not accurate.

At first glance, these criteria seem almost too rigid. One may feel that no man could ever meet them all. In fact, the application of these criteria is somewhat subjective. For example, what may be "just" in one person's opinion may not be considered "just" to others. Still, the overall picture is of a man with leadership gifts, teaching gifts, and the moral character necessary to assume the responsibility of leading God's church along with others of like calling. To use our S.H.A.P.E. paradigm, he should have:

Spiritual Gifts: Leadership, hospitality, teaching.
Heart: To lead, serve, care, and oversee.
Abilities: Parenting, stewardship, etc.
Personality: Patient, not pushy, etc.
Experience: Good reputation, good family life, etc.

In addition, he must have a reputation of good Christian living. Remember, an Elder's job is to equip the saints—that's you and me—for ministry. His job is not to DO ministry for us!

Application

So how do we use this information? First, it's important to go back and look up and read all of the scripture in this booklet. Study them in their context and pray over them. Only then are we ready to apply the truths they contain and avoid the unnecessary misunderstandings and/or division over this issue. Next, we should begin to ask God to reveal who he has placed in our midst to fulfill this office. Ephesians 4, 1 Corinthians 12, and Romans 12 all seem to imply that God will ALWAYS place proper leaders/Elders among his people. The question is NOT whether we have Elders in our church, but where they are.

Pray and study over the qualifications in Titus 1 and 1 Timothy 3. As names come to mind, write them down and pray over them asking God to clarify to us whether or not he has called these men to the office of Elder in his body, the church. Remember that while functions and gifts can differ, the ordination or calling of Elder remains the same (2 Peter 5:1). The Elders, much like the congregation, all work together using their various gifts to lead the congregation according to God's will.

Our next step as a church, is when asked, to nominate anyone we feel may be called to the office of Elder and pray for our current leadership that they will have the wisdom and guidance needed to make the final selections. There is no set number of Elders who must be found. Still, we want to recognize and use all whom the Lord has chosen. Are we going to immediately place these men in authority over everything and replace our Church Board? No! We need to find them first and have them serve alongside our deacons on the Deacon Board. Eventually, we will have to review our organizational structure in view of scripture, but we will do that with patience, lots of input and time.

Another bridge we'll eventually need to cross is the whole subject of ordination. Ordination of deacons and Elders is, as we've seen in the scriptures referenced above, a biblical concept. Ordination is like baptism in that it simply acknowledges what the Holy Spirit has ALREADY done. By ordaining someone as an Elder or a deacon, we're showing that we recognize the fruits needed for that office. What's important about ordination is that it is NOT a temporary thing. If we ordain an Elder, we are recognizing the persons' call to that office for life. We might assign him to other responsibilities at times, but he's still an Elder as long as he continues to meet the biblical criteria. He doesn't cease to be an Elder after a term of office on the "Elder Board" is completed, etc. Therefore, before we ordain someone, we want to allow for questioning of the individual by the congregation as a whole, etc.

For now, let's seek the Lord as to who the Elders are among us and then begin to use them in service with our deacons. This will also help us understand the distinctions between these two offices (See our booklet, "Just What IS a Deacon Anyway?" for more information on the differences between deacons and Elders in the Bible). It is our belief that the addition of Elders to our body will help our church better fulfill God's call by accomplishing His purposes both now, and in the future (Matthew 22:37-40, Matthew 28:19-20, and others).

Appendix iii

Note: This article appeared in our church newsletter during our transition toward a more Elder-led structure. It is reprinted here for clarity and/or for use as you see fit...

<u>Just What IS a Deacon Anyway?</u>
...A Study Guide

As with our booklet on Elders, perhaps the best place to start is to discuss what a Deacon is NOT. A New Testament Deacon is NOT:

- Someone who meets all physical, spiritual, and administrative church needs.
- An "Elder-wannabe."
- The "top dog" in church leadership.
- Some ONLY concerned with "spiritual issues."
- Someone who is just eligible or available to serve because we must "fill a slot."

The biggest challenge we face is that, since we have not had Elders in our congregation, the role of Deacon is often confused with that of Elder. In fact, our current Deacons carry responsibilities and have a mix of gifts that make them what I would call, "dElders" or "eldcons." In other words, they're somewhere in between the two biblical offices. Therefore, the first thing we should cover here is that Deacons are not Elders and Elders are not necessarily Deacons either.

Biblically, Deacons are NOT primarily concerned with spiritual issues. While there is overlap, Deacons are not the primary leaders of the congregation. While leaders, their concerns are typically different and their qualifications are also somewhat unique as compared to Elders. Just as Elders, Deacons are ordained when God calls them to this office (see "Just What IS and Elder..." booklet/article for more information on ordination).

Historical Background

The Greek word often translated "Deacon" actually means "servant." In fact, that's the simplest definition. A Deacon is a servant. This is clearly demonstrated in the choice and ordination of the first Deacons in Acts 6. Let's look at this in some detail:

1 And in those days, when the number of the disciples was multiplied, there arose a murmuring of the Grecians against the Hebrews, because their widows were neglected in the daily ministration. 2 Then the twelve called the multitude of the disciples unto them, and said, It is not reason that we should leave the word of God, and serve tables. 3 Wherefore, brethren, look ye out among you seven men of honest report, full of the Holy Ghost and wisdom, whom we may appoint over this business. 4 But we will give ourselves continually to prayer, and to the ministry of the word. 5 And the saying pleased the whole multitude: and they chose Stephen, a man full of faith and of the Holy Ghost, and Philip, and Prochorus, and Nicanor, and Timon, and Parmenas, and Nicolas a proselyte of Antioch: 6 Whom they set before the apostles: and when they had prayed, they laid their hands on them. 7 And the word of God increased; and the number of the disciples multiplied in Jerusalem greatly; and a great company of the priests were obedient to the faith. (Acts 6:1-7, KJV)

These men were servants, but full of the Holy Spirit and the gift of wisdom to make the choices and decisions necessary to solve this conflict. The mention of wisdom reminds us of Solomon who is resolved physical disputes between God's people (See 1 Kings 3:16-27).

What is especially interesting here is that the REASON for the ordination of Deacons was NOT a spiritual need! It was a physical/financial issue that was taking the apostles/Elders away from Their primary duties—prayer, teaching, etc. here we see the first difference in focus between the office of Elder and that of Deacon—Deacons are primarily managers/leaders over physical and financial issues within the church. They don't teach or deal with other ministry needs. What scripture indicates is a difference in FOCUS or PRIORITY as compared to Elders. Deacons were in effect, the "middle management" of the church, who had special concern for business and administrative issues. They worked closely with the Elders (Philippians 1:1), but their roles were different (see "Just What IS an Elder Anyway," for more information).

Deacons are called by God to this office. They should have spiritual gifts of mercy, service, helps, etc; a heart for meeting needs, abilities to steward and manage, a personality suitable to the local church, and experiences that show God's hand on their lives. It should also be clear that the Deacons help equip the members for ministry. They don't DO the entire ministry themselves (Ephesians 4:11-16). Another interesting point here is that the Deacons were chosen by the congregation and then ordained by the Apostles/Elders. They were not "elected," per se, but rather nominated by the congregation in Jerusalem. Because they were chosen and ordained based on character and spiritual gifting, just as with Elders, they did not serve a temporary "term" of office. While their roles changed, (as with Phillip and Stephen in the following chapters), their ordained office apparently did not.

Deaconesses

Another interesting difference between Deacons and Elders is the use of women in leadership roles in the early church. While general differences between men and women apply as do Paul's admonitions about women generally not overseeing men (1 Timothy 2:21), the role of Deacon and the role of Deaconesses are pretty much the same. One biblical example of a Deaconesses is Phoebe (Romans 16:1), who Paul commends as a servant of many. Some scholars believe that the admonitions Paul makes regarding "their wives" in the list of Deacon qualifications (see below) are actually qualifications given to Deaconesses in the early church. Be that as it may, the existence of Deaconesses in the church and the view of theirs as an office of "middle management" responsibility over physical needs in the church, is practically unquestioned. While we may not see the evidence of women being ordained as Deaconesses, we DO see precedent for having

Deaconess leaders in administrative roles helping serve, assist, and care for the local church.

Qualifications

Let's look at the primary list of requirements for Deacons from I Timothy 3.

> *8 Likewise must the Deacons be grave, not double tongued, not given to much wine, not greedy of filthy lucre; 9 Holding the mystery of the faith in a pure conscience. 10 And let these also first be proved; then let them use the office of a Deacon, being found blameless. 11 Even so must their wives be grave, not slanderers, sober, faithful in all things. 12 Let the Deacons be the husbands of one wife, ruling their children and their own houses well. 13 For they that have used the office of a Deacon well purchase to themselves a good degree, and great boldness in the faith which is in Christ Jesus (1 Tim 3:8-13, KJV)*

Here's the list in another form including the qualifications mentioned in Acts 6:

- Gift of Mercy
- Respectable

- Sincere
- Doctrinally Sound and Consistent
- Scripturally bound to one wife.
- Gift of Wisdom
- Stewardship Abilities
- Helps/Service Gifts
- Not misusing alcohol or drugs
- Not greedy
- Having a good track record of service
- A good husband/father
- A heart for meeting needs

Deacons were to know the word, but don't have the requirement of being able to teach it necessarily. Also of note is their track record of service. Deacons were tested. If they weren't willing to serve without the office, they weren't truly called to the office of Deacon. Their duties were primarily physical in nature probably made "on the job training" and testing more feasible.

Application

Application of these truths as with the biblical teachings regarding Elders, can only be made after study of the scriptures involved. Please prayerfully review each passage quoted herein in its context. Consider how our current Deacons and Deaconesses are filling these roles. Ask God to show us if any changes are needed in our approach.

It would seem that the primary areas of concerns regarding our church's current use of the office of Deacon/Deaconess would be as follows:

- The question of ordination versus "term of service" for Deacons and Elders.
- The physical, administrative and financial authority given to these folks in scripture.
- The separation of Elders from Deacons in our structure and the use of both offices.

For now, our primary task should be to clearly designate and distinguish between the Elders and Deacons in our congregation and on our Deacon Board. Next, we should consider how Deacons are called and ordained such that a Deacon never ceases to be called a Deacon, even if he isn't serving on the Deacon Board during a sabbatical of other circumstance. It also seems clear that we should try to give more respect and attention to the proper use of Deaconesses in our midst. Eventually, the role of the Deacon Board as opposed to an Elder Board, and the oversight of physical resources such as church property and finances, all need to be evaluated as part of our church structure. Still, these things will come in time and with patience.

Recommended Reading

Rainer, Thom S., Eric Geiger. *Simple Church, B&H Publishing Group, 2006, ISBN 0805443908.*

Cymbala, Jim, Merrill, Dean. *Fresh Wind, Fresh Fire.* Zondervan 2003, ISBN 0310251532

Olson, David T., The American Church in Crisis, Tyndale, 2005. ISBN 13:978-0-310-27713-2

Hybels, Bill, Mittleberg, Mark, Strobel, Lee. *The Contagious Christian*, Zondervan, 2007,ISBN 0310257875

Southerland, Dan. *Transitioning*, Zondervan, 1999, ISBN 031024681

Warren, Rick. *Purpose-Driven Church*, Zondervan 1995, ISBN 0310201063

Stetzer, Ed. *Planting Missional Churches, B&H Publishing Group, 2006, ISBN* 0805443703

Barna, George. *Revolution,* Tyndale House Publishers, 2005, ISBN 1414307586

Colson, Chuck, Pearcey, Nancy. *The Christian in Today's Culture: Developing a Biblical Worldview,* Tyndale, 2001, ISBN 0842355871

Footnotes

1. Butler Bass, Diana, "The Real Decline of Churches," www. belief.net, July 20, 2009.

2. David T. Olson, *The American Church in Crisis,* (Grand Rapids, MI, Zondervan,2008), page 16.

3. Grossman, Cathy Lynn, "Most Religious Groups Have Lost Ground," *USA Today, March 9, 2009*.

4.   Barna, George, *Revolution*, (Wheaton, IL, Tyndale 2005), Pages 29-40.
Southerland, Dan. *Transitioning*, Zondervan, 1999, Entire book/story.

5. Stetzer, Ed, "Finding New Life for Struggling Churches," SBC Life (www.sbclife.net), February 2004.

6.Olson, Pages 92-116.

7. Ibid., Pages 92-116.

8. Ibid., Pages 92-116.

9. Ibid., Pages 92-116.

10. "Ee-Taow, and Next Chapter DVD," www.ntmbooks.com.

11. Rainer, Thom S., Eric Geiger. *Simple Church, B&H Publishing Group, 2006, ISBN 0805443908.*

12. Asia Times, www.atimes.com, "Christianity Finds a Fulcrum in Asia," August, 2007.

13. Cymbala, Jim, Merrill, Dean. *Fresh Wind, Fresh Fire.* Zondervan 2003, ISBN 0310251532

14. Author Unknown, "Don't Quit," www.thedontquitpoem. com.

Breinigsville, PA USA
20 March 2011
257978BV00001B/10/P